Becoming Tarden

Paperback edition. First published in September 2009.
Confiscated by the Dutch government January 4, 2010.

Copy edited by Ella Christopherson.
Cover and book design by Emily Lessard.

Printed by Print Craft, Minneapolis, Minnesota.

Jill Magid

Becoming Tarden

2010

Contents

For the former Committee Head, who gave me permission to call him by his name.

The secret itself is much more beautiful than its revelation.

—The report for the AIVD on the subject of its face

I am presenting the book disbound. I sliced the joints along its shoulders, pulled its body from its spine, and laid it under glass.

You may take the body of the book. I will keep the prologue and the epilogue. These parts support the body, before and after my commission, and do not include my sources.

The book, *Becoming Tarden,* is a memoir of our involvement. I had dreams of publishing it as my first novel. You are its only reader. Seize it. Strip it. Hold it in your building and seal it under glass. I comply.

Your Author,

Jill Magid

Jill Magid

—From a letter to the Director of the Organization dated August 26, 2009, submitted with the first edition of *Becoming Tarden* in its complete and unredacted form.

Epilogue

I title the exhibition for my commission "Article 12." The artworks have been lifted from my notebooks. Excerpts from *Cockpit* are hung along a wall that pierces through the gallery. My list of directives scrolls down from the ceiling and onto the floor. Eighteen prints describe my sources' faces. A red neon installation warns that I can burn them. My notebooks are closed and locked under glass. They will be surrendered.

The day before the opening, the Organization sends a group of agents to the gallery to review and approve my work. There are four of them: my Committee Head, an older woman whose position I do not know, a senior spokesman from the communications department, and the head of buildings and security. I take them on a tour of the exhibition and present the works within it. The spokesman reads aloud every neon word as well as those in the prints, as if he were performing them.

Before they leave, I give my Committee Head a rough copy of my report, my interviews with my sources, for them to redact.

My exhibition opens to the public the following day. The four agents who approved it attend the event.

In the following weeks, "Article 12" receives extensive press in a number of local publications as well as every national newspaper in Holland, including a front-page story in *de Volkskrant*, continued in the arts section.

On May 17, 2008, my Committee Head calls me in New York to inform me that the redactions are complete. She will need to meet with my advisor before they can be released to me.

A quarter of your report has been censored. Does that scare you?

I admit that it does.

We removed all references to the identities of your sources. There were a lot of them. You know that, though, because you wrote it.

I tell her that, in the meantime, I will finish the manuscript.

There is more?

I assure her that my additions concern my personal experience, giving the interviews context without affecting their content.

We will need to see the final version of the manuscript, no matter what the changes are. A second screening of the document creates extra work for us. Now we'll have to redact it twice.

I arrive in Amsterdam on Tuesday June 3 and call my advisor. He says he has bad news. The Director of the Organization is suddenly involved with my assignment. He called an emergency meeting with my advisor the day before, while I was in transit. He brought a lawyer representing the Organization and the spokesman from the communications department who had approved my show.

In the emergency meeting, the Director announced that the Organization will no longer permit my exhibition to travel. It plans to confiscate the eighteen prints in the gallery and any forthcoming editions. He wants me to discontinue work on my book and agree not to publish it. The Organization is threatening to seize my computer and wipe its hard disks clean of any material connected with the project. If I refuse to comply, they'll take me to court.

We plan to reconvene at the Agency to discuss these demands.

On Thursday June 5, I arrive at the Agency for a briefing with its lawyer, my advisor, and his boss, the advisor coordinator. The lawyer explains that the contract for my commission is between the Agency—not the Organization—and me.

One hour later, my advisor collects the Director of the Organization from downstairs. The rest of us relocate to a conference room, bare of windows, and wait for them.

We hear voices in the hallway. My advisor leads the Director inside. He has strawberry blond hair that would be curly if he was younger or he wore it longer, but it's short and thinning on his crown. He wears a plain blue suit and no tie. It takes me a long time to remember his face. The Organization's lawyer, who the Director said he would not be bringing, enters after him. She wears blue eye shadow, her highlighted blonde hair tied back in a pigtail, and a black dress suit that is too tight across the buttons. Instead of the spokesman who had approved my show, there is another agent from his department who looks somewhat like him. He is much younger, with curly dark hair, a round face and round glasses, big teeth, and pale skin. He and the lawyer sit huddled together at one end of the table to the left of the Director, who sits across from me.

My advisor begins by saying he is not exactly sure why we are meeting since the director of his agency has agreed to support my commission.

The Organization's Director raises his index finger. *I can begin.*

There are two reasons why we are meeting here. One is the exhibition and, more specifically, the objects that are in it. The second is the manuscript.

My advisor immediately clarifies these issues: The Agency is responsible for the artworks and the book is mine, to be handled separately to the commission. He is happy to discuss any issues related to the artwork, but the book is beyond his control.

The Director and the communications agent look frustrated. *We agreed to a show but never to a book. The book should not exist as it is not in the show.* The Director asks me to admit, since my advisor won't, that the book and the artworks are the same project and thus should be covered by the same contract.

My advisor speaks on my behalf. *They come from the same experience, but they are different works.*

The Director responds to me. *The material we gave you was for the commission. That did not include a book.*

My advisor counters. *Where does it say it can't?*

The Director changes his strategy, keeping his gaze on me. *The agents you met with were very upset about how they were represented in your report.*

My mouth drops, and I shake my head. They were never supposed to read the book before it was redacted.

The communications agent leans toward me, gesturing with his hands while he speaks. *You don't know the redacting process like we do. Redacting is not done by just one person; it is the responsibility of a whole team. We brought the sections of the book that refer to particular agents to him or her to read because that is what we do. We ask them, "Can you recognize yourself here?" and, "What else do you want removed?" You don't know how our process works.*

I consider the way Miranda III explained the process to me and how it was nothing like this.

We have already redacted three quarters of the text.

My Committee Head told me that one quarter had been censored due to source protection.

Our methodology must also be considered. The first reader redacted any information that revealed your sources, then it went to another reader, and then to more readers, and now it has withered away to a series of white and empty pages.

My advisor asks them to define their issue with the artworks.

We were surprised by the prints that describe our agents' faces. They were not included in Jill's exhibition proposal.

My advisor disagrees. *You were informed about the prints and your committee head approved them.* He refers to my proposal:

I Can Burn Your Face, *neon and nonsbestos, variable sizes.*

Descriptions of each source I have interviewed (18) will be used to make the works. I will transcribe the text on nonsbestos, a paper used for neon patternmaking. Phrases from these descriptions will be bent into neon. The process of bending glass on nonsbestos burns the letters into the paper. Both *the burned patterns* and *the neon words will be installed in the exhibition.*
(His emphasis)

I explain that the only differences between my proposal and its realization are the title and the materials used: The set of prints has its own title and, rather than burning the text on nonsbestos, I pressed them into paper.

The Director shakes his head and limply waves his hand. *We don't care about the paper.* He looks tired and older than before, as if he is aging at the table. He inhales deeply, then looks at me sternly, and slices the air with his palm. *We want this to end.*

It had ended, and then you called this meeting.

This is a business meeting, Jill.

Yes. This is a meeting.

No, it is a business *meeting.*

I am unclear of your distinction.

This is business, Jill. This is not art. I do not want to be a part of your book.

I think but do not say, You are writing my epilogue as you speak.

The communications agent moves in. *The book threatens the safety of your sources.*

I had always planned to protect them. I gave the book to my Committee Head to redact, as we had agreed when the book was first discussed as a way to fulfill the commission. I am trying to uphold the integrity of our initial agreement—I make my sources unidentifiable, I separate who they are from what they say.

The Director smiles paternally. *This is not about your integrity, Jill. We are not attacking that.*

And I do not feel it's threatened. I have been forthright throughout this process. I did exactly what you asked me to do. It is your organization that has changed the rules since Monday.

The Director becomes visibly angry. His face deepens in color and he spits when he speaks. *The deal was that you return everything when your research was complete, and your commission was an exhibition—not a book.*

There was never a discussion of what I would return to you, only that I would protect my sources with your organization's help. That is why I submitted the manuscript.

The Director refers back to our meeting in his office. *The deal then was that, when the exhibition was over, you would give everything you collected and made back to the Organization.*

I correct him. We did not discuss that in your office. I came to you to ask permission to be trained, which you denied. I sought permission, one year later, to give my notebooks to the Organization sealed in a glass vitrine. I proposed this as an artwork, to be displayed temporarily in the exhibition and then permanently in your new building. I wanted your institution to recognize me as part of its history. If I was a real agent of the Organization and my term was over, I would be required to relinquish all my original files. They would be placed in a box marked with my vetting number and stored in your archive.

He pauses before returning to a previously tried strategy. *Your sources feel betrayed. They feel used, and are scared for their safety. Your prints expose them. Someone on the outside, who knows our organization well enough, could recognize them.*

The Organization was informed of the prints in my proposal. It then had them reviewed and approved before the exhibition opened six weeks ago.

People within the Organization can recognize one another.

I described how I saw them, not the information they gave me.

The sources can recognize themselves.

It is not my responsibility to shield them from themselves.

The communications agent adds, *It is not just your sources you must protect, but the methods of the Organization. You describe them in the book.*

19

My advisor breaks in. *What if the commission had ended and, one year from now, Jill decided to write a book about her experience? What then?*

His question seems to further deplete the Director, whose voice sounds strained. *We cannot stop her from writing a book—a fiction—but this is different. This book is based on the interviews she did for the commission. The deal was that her notebooks be returned to us and closed forever once her assignment was over.*

My advisor leans forward. *I have to interrupt here—what is this deal to which you keep referring? Is it written down anywhere? It's not part of the contract.*

The Director clenches his fists and turns to me again. *If you will agree not to write the book—*

I can no longer contain myself. Look, there is going to be a book. I am trying to uphold my end of our agreement—I gave the Organization my report in April to redact under the terms of source protection. You have already told me today that I do not know how to redact it properly myself. If you do not cooperate and redact my manuscript, it is you who are making your agents vulnerable. I am writing this book—with or without your collaboration. But I would prefer your cooperation.

The Director's face turns blood red, heightened by the golden hue of his thinning hair. His shoulders sag forward and his fists, which he had clenched up near his face, relax and fall slowly to the table like dead leaves in still air. He says quietly, *Only fourteen of your prints were on display in the exhibition. We would like to see the other four before they travel.*

For a moment we are all speechless. The lawyers, who have been inactive, write furiously. *Before they travel...* Tension releases from the room like an uncorked bottle. I arch my back and roll my hair into a loose bun. The advisor coordinator interlocks his fingers and rests his hands in his lap. My advisor, who has stretched his upper body out across the table, remains there motionless. The Director continues. *If we cooperate, will you put the book in the vitrine, Jill?* It takes a moment for me to hear what he is actually saying rather than how he is saying it. He uses my name, no longer condescending but beseeching. It is the first time he has truly asked me a question, one person to another, on equal ground. I had never sought to equal him. He was so immense that he was constant, a steady force, an *idea* emanating from the center of the Building that could not be influenced, only approached, observed, and felt. If the locus of power is fluid, the reflection in a mirror that changes with its context, then I must be changing, too.

The communications agent is mid-sentence, portraying the prints as teetering on the edge rather than going beyond it, whereas the book—

My advisor interrupts him. *What are you proposing?*

He directs his answer to me. *We want you to think of the book as an object of art. We will redact it and put it inside the vitrine with your notebooks where it will remain, permanently.*

Your want me to put it under glass so that it will no longer function as a book but as a sculpture?

Yes. He blinks his eyes rapidly. *It becomes an object of art.*

The Director follows this in a soft, imploring voice. *Will you consider that, Jill?*

Power is a set of relations. I learned that phrase in an anthropology class at Cornell University titled "Culture and Power." I used it several times in my term papers, but never truly understood it until now. Power is a set of relations, and he just gave his power to me. I know my answer, but choose not to tell him.

Instead I say this: I am tired. A lot has been put out on the table and I need to think about it. I ask him to consider giving me a copy of the redactions the Organization has already done so that I can make an informed decision.

My advisor volunteers to mediate further discussions between the Organization and myself once I return to New York. The Director does not object but says he prefers to speak with me directly. I tell him that is fine and suggest he come to Brooklyn. He hunches his back and forces a laugh, like the aged father who was once a disciplinarian but has since folded under his own weak bones, and I feel bad to see him lose the very thing that made me fear him because without fear the world is boundless, without a frame to hold it. If nothing is hidden, nothing can be found and nothing can be lost, and yet I am lost, we are lost, as we are also free. I drop back in my chair, flooded with relief and the profound exhilaration of autonomy, to be quickly replaced by a sadness at having nothing left to fear.

On the way back from The Hague, my advisor drives while his boss smokes a joint in the front seat of the car. He is singing "Wild Thing" to a different song that has a similar beat before he turns to me in the backseat and says, *What I find so fascinating is the philosophical position that you and the Organization are in. This is a question of intellectual property rights: How far can they go to erase your experience? They want you to return three years of memories and encounters and never refer to them again. Besides conducting surgery on your brain, how can they succeed? You cannot be the same person after this assignment; it has profoundly affected you and altered your perception of the world. How can they remove that? It's stupid.* He turns back to face the windshield and exhales an earthy cloud of smoke, out the window and over the highway that leads us back to Amsterdam.

Prologue

Living in Amsterdam in the spring of 2004, I received a letter from a senior advisor to the Netherlands' chief government architect. Enclosed was a job description, translated from Dutch. The Government Buildings Agency was hiring on behalf of the De Algemene Inlichtingen en Veilingheidsdienst, or the Dutch secret service. The Organization had doubled in size over recent years due to the new wave of global terrorism and was thus moving to a larger building. As a government project funded with public money, federal law required a percentage of the building's total budget be used to commission a new onsite artwork. The Agency's mission was to appoint someone whose work would support the mission of the Organization.

The Organization's reluctance to commission an artist was clear from the document, which excited me even more. It described its task as to protect the interests of the nation by researching groups and individuals, both domestic and international, which pose a threat to the democratic order of the state. Society, it wrote, expects the Organization to know what those threats include. At the same time, citizens require legal protection against techniques used by the Organization that invade the personal domain, such as audio and physical surveillance. The

Organization acknowledged that just how far it is permitted to go in fulfilling its task without compromising the cornerstones of Dutch society—openness, democracy, and civil rights for all—is constantly in question. "Sometimes," the letter concluded, "the information that is assembled cannot be made public. Where possible the organization tries to be open."

Applications should include a resume, mission statement, and examples of relevant work.

In sending me the letter, the senior advisor had clearly recognized what I did: This job was perfect for me. It was the logical next step in my career, which had come to involve an experiential investigation of secrecy and government institutions—often by my infiltrating them. I sat down at my improvised desk in the canal house at which I was staying and prepared my application. I wrote it in a voice with which the Government Buildings Agency and the Organization would identify, or even think they might be able to exploit—a skill I had learned from experience.

The letter arrived just as I was planning to leave the country permanently. My desire to work with the Organization put that move on hold. I called the friend who was subletting my old apartment. We had agreed that if living with my boyfriend did not work out and I remained in Holland, I could reclaim my flat. I suggested he start making other arrangements, just in case.

Three weeks later, the Agency advisor informed me that I'd passed the first screening. One step closer to the Organization, I decided to wait it out. I notified my subletter. He had until the end of the month to vacate.

Meanwhile, I stayed on living with my boyfriend. He was

from Amsterdam, and had lived there all his life. He knew the city intimately and, due to his job at a new media arts foundation, was deeply enmeshed in its hacker subculture. I had been seeing him for a while before I left for Liverpool to work on a commission for the city's biennial exhibition. In my absence, he'd taken a flat on Spuistraat while his was being renovated. It was a duplex on the top floors of a large canal house, above an Internet café. At the front of the café was a shop where customers could buy postcards and stamps, candy, magazines about cars, and plastic toys for children.

At night, the storefronts across from his apartment became showcases for prostitution, signaled by red fluorescent tube lights mounted to the tops of the windows. They hummed with an unearthly glow, augmented by black bulbs installed deeper in the spaces. When the viewing stalls were empty of their male clientele, the women pressed their tattooed bodies up against the glass, sometimes flicking their tongues and wiggling their hips but more often than not looking bored. From our third floor window, I could peer down into theirs and see the white bedsheets and porcelain sinks radiating phosphorescent purple.

Late at night, I would watch the lone figures prowling the street in front of our house. They emerged from the narrow alleyways between buildings and occasionally collected in small, agitated groups near the church, as if they were plotting something. Some were dark men in leather jackets with gelled-back hair who walked with a sense of purpose. Others, in old or crumpled suits, looked lost, drunk, self-conscious, dejected. They moved at a slower pace, hovering at each window before choosing a door.

The door to each prostitute's room was the threshold of a void. I would watch as a man approached it, I would see it open

27

slightly as the price was negotiated, then open further to allow him in. The door would shut and the curtain would close. After a time, he'd come out the door again, legs first, his upper body leaning in as he said goodbye or paid the fee. The door would shut behind him and the curtain reopen. There she was again.

There was a dreariness to the humdrum of these nightly charades that I found comforting. Its repetition soothed me when sleep would not come, which at the time was often. Because of this, the apartment had become one of my favorite places I had stayed in the city, and I had stayed in many. My relationship was at its most simple then, too. Living together in a temporary house afforded a temporary commitment, unburdened by future obligations. I focused on developing my research and preparing my presentation for the Organization, which I worked on daily, interspersed with short walks and bike rides through the city.

On June 22, 2004, I was asked to meet with the Organization's selection committee at the Government Buildings Agency office in The Hague. The committee was already assembled when I arrived—they'd been screening other candidates that morning. The interviews were being conducted in a semiprivate room closed off from the rest of the office by soundproofed glass walls. The desks closest to the room were vacant; I assumed they'd been cleared. The committee, seated around a black oval table, numbered around fifteen people. All the men were in business suits; most of the women wore mid-length skirts or dress pants with silky blouses buttoned to various heights. The amount of cleavage revealed depended on the women's ages, which ranged greatly. The younger committee members greeted me with a smile; the elders barely nodded.

The advisor dimmed the lights. Using carefully selected images, I traced the stages of my development. I began with a slide that showed my hand holding a thin rod with a small mirror attached to its end, cut in the shape of a skyscraper. The mirror reflects the Empire State Building. It looks as if I'm holding the actual building. The next image is of a stiletto shoe that I fitted with a small security camera attached to its heel. On the underside of the shoe sole is a wireless transmitter, about the size of a stick of gum. The following slide displays the transmitted image from the camera: a view up the side of my body, distorted by the camera's wide-angle lens, with the city of Boston in the background. I am as tall as the buildings. The next slide shows a similarly distorted image of my body through a surveillance camera lens. Unauthorized, I'd hacked into a university's security system and projected a live video stream from a camera beneath my clothes. The following image was taken in Amsterdam. It is a detailed shot of an outdoor security camera that I covered in rhinestones. The next image is of myself, at the top of a ladder that is leaning against the facade of the headquarters of the Amsterdam police department. I am covering the building's security cameras with jewels. The next image is of one of the police administrators (I wonder if anyone on the selection committee recognized him?) who had hired me for the job, admiring a glittering camera from the sidewalk. Lastly, I showed images from my time in Liverpool where I had recently worked with the police department and its citywide CCTV system. I am the subject of video stills taken with the police's cameras, always wearing the same red trench coat. The stills are rich in color and cinematic in scope. The detailed shots of my face feel intimate. I let those linger. Over these images, I described to the committee my process of working closely with government institutions to identify with them personally and locate their human side. I inferred that I could do the same for the Organization.

I then thanked the committee and the advisor escorted me out of the room. Before attending to the next candidate, he squeezed my arm and whispered, *That was very good*.

A few days later, I was strolling through Dam Square with a former classmate of mine who was visiting the city on business. As we discussed the pros and cons of living in Europe versus the States, I got a call from the Agency. The advisor notified me that the Organization had offered me the commission. I grabbed my friend by the shirtsleeve and silently mouthed, Yes! The advisor explained that he would continue to work with me on this assignment on behalf of the Agency as a mediator between the Organization and myself. I had until the end of the year to prepare my angle and outline exactly what I proposed to do for the Organization.

My friend suggested we celebrate in the first bar we came upon. We spotted a *bruine kroeg* or 'brown bar'—the Dutch name for their traditional bars made of dark wood. Upon entering we found that a group of loud, inebriated British men, the kind that arrive on the ferry and like to sing while they drink, had overtaken the bar. I didn't mind—their festive mood fit mine. Over white beers with lemon, my friend and I marveled at how ideal the assignment was for me and how it had provided me with a reason to stay abroad.

I reclaimed my old apartment and loosened ties with my boyfriend. My lack of commitment to our relationship and to

Amsterdam wore him thin. My apartment was in the Jordan, across the canal from the Anne Frank house that now, from the outside, looks more like a modern steel-clad condominium than a once-innocuous residence of hiding. I had lived there for a little over a year before subletting it to my friend while I was in Liverpool. I had planned to return to Amsterdam only to gather my belongings but realized, once back from Liverpool, that I'd rather develop my work in a city where I had already been living, without the hassle of moving again. I prefer to have a specific reason to relocate—a job or a project to follow—than to leave simply because I want to.

My apartment in the Jordan occupied the top two thirds of a fairytale house, three-and-a-half stories high. The space was narrow and extremely small, roughly three hundred square meters including the stairs, kitchen, living area, and the attic where I slept. In the tightly curved stairwell between the kitchen and the living area—which contained a bathroom with a shower and toilet, a sink, an old pea-green armchair, a large wooden desk that barely fit, and a freestanding hanging rod for my clothes—most people had to crook their neck. My body fit perfectly.

The front door was tucked away in a courtyard, accessible from the street only via a narrow gap in a vine-covered brick wall. It's an historic site, once part of a convent. Groups of tourists would often wander into the courtyard to take pictures. They'd stand at its center, under the lone tree that reached up to shade my kitchen window for the few months it had leaves. With their guidebooks open to passages with which I'd become familiar, they'd read aloud in various languages the history of the complex, reciting the inscription on the clamshell wall fountain that no longer worked and was usually filled with trash. From there, they'd lift their gaze to the second-floor landing—on a level with my kitchen window—where a statue of a nun offered up her palms to bless those of us below. The neighbor's ginger cat that often crawled in my bedroom window at night liked to sit by her feet and watch the sightseers. They would peer inside the apartments whenever tenants opened their doors. Mine particularly shocked them. My front door opened abruptly onto a steep staircase akin to a ladder. Every time I returned from traveling I'd suffer through a few days of bruised shins before getting back into the habit of climbing the stairs sideways to avoid banging my leg on the next step. Besides the tourists, it was a very quiet place, housing students and scholars from abroad, as I had been when I first moved there. All of the apartments overlooking the courtyard were single occupancy residencies that attracted people like me who preferred to be left alone when at home, consumed with their studies. It was the perfect place to think and feel removed from the city while living in its heart.

I resettled easily and quickly got to work. The Agency had sent me a large parcel with the Organization's renovation plans for its new building, as well as computer-generated drawings of its completed design. As with all of its commissions, the Agency expected me to propose an artwork for a specific location within the Building. I had no intention of importing something I'd made in the studio. I wanted to be intimately involved with the Organization, to penetrate it. I studied the Building's blueprints to gain insight into its administrative structure, but to no avail. Originally designed as the Ministry of Education, Culture and Science, the construction was a conglomerate of hexagonal clusters, like the cross section of a honeycomb. If there was a central point within the Building from which power would emanate, it was impossible to locate from its architecture.

Also enclosed in the parcel were a number of thin booklets published by the Organization about its work. Their titles included *About Positions Involving Confidentiality and Security Investigations, Recruitment for the Jihad in the Netherlands, Terrorism at the Start of the 21st Century*, and my favorite, *Espionage and Security Risks: Invisible but Still Existing*. I was inspired by their opaque, poetic use of language. I copied terms such as "vulnerability analysis," "declaration of non-objection," and "risk orientation" into my notebook and compiled a list of questions about the Organization's methodology to present to the committee.

I visited the Building on November 17, December 12, and again on the 22, accompanied by the Agency advisor. We met with the Committee Head—who became deeply interested in my practice—and various committee members. I posed to them the questions from my notebooks. I asked them to explain how confidentiality and security screenings were conducted, and to clarify the differences between security clearance levels A, B, and C. I wanted to know what security level I would be granted if I became an agent, and what kind of access that would allow me; how citizens go about applying the Freedom of Information Act to see their classified files; and if the Organization would keep a file on me now that I was working for them. I asked about surveillance practices and searches of homes, and what they referred to as "closed objects." I'd read that suspect objects were sometimes removed discreetly from private residences, analyzed, and reinserted back into place within three days. I asked how the Organization trained agents to conduct these searches, what tools were used, how the results were analyzed and documented, and if they would teach me how to do it. Many of my questions were passed over without being answered. They responded whenever they could.

Inside the Building, I was never left alone. If I used the bathroom before entering the conference room, whomever I was meeting would stand outside the door. The advisor commented that this seemed suspect, as if I was wiretapping myself.

On my last visit, the Committee Head showed me the Organization's collection of "dead letter boxes"—objects that had been used to hide things. There was a block of cement containing a roll of film that could only be seen with an X-ray, attaché cases with false backs and hidden pockets, shoe heels with cavities in which to hide devices. They were old, beautiful, analog. I wondered aloud how the Organization did this now, with so many digital options. *It is difficult*, he admitted.

Meanwhile, I spoke with those on the outside who eyed the Organization with suspicion. I asked people around town what they thought of the service, whether they approved of it and, if not, why they didn't. I delved into the service's past practices. I located activists who had dedicated their lives to watching its every move in the hopes of countering them. I'd been in Amsterdam long enough to have made useful connections. I knew prominent academics in the city's universities as well as some infamous hackers. I told a select few about my commission. Networks opened up; people emerged. Many who agreed to meet with me had their own agendas. A few wanted me to wear a wire the next time I went to the Building. I listened to them all without judgment, careful to remain open to who or whatever the Organization might be beyond their speculations.

I wondered if the Organization knew I was doing this behind its back. I fantasized it was aware of my every move. I visited a man at his house on the outskirts of the city, where he kept a small workshop full of phones he had hacked to sneak an ear into the Building. He also rewired people's phones so that agents could not tap them. I wondered if anyone was really listening in on them or if they were simply fantasizing like me.

Back in the city center, I wandered into The American Book Center on Spuistraat, not far from the canal house at which I'd stayed. I had lived in Amsterdam for four and a half years but still did not speak the language. Preferring to remain a perpetual visitor, I hadn't tried to learn. I headed to the fiction section, picked up a book by a familiar author, and skimmed the commentary inside. The reviewer compared the novel to those of Jerzy Kosinksi. I had never heard of him, so I moved to the K section and scanned his titles on the shelf. I reached for one called *Cockpit*. The back cover described the novel's protagonist as a former operative for a mysterious government agency, living a life free of identity, erased from all dossiers and transcripts. As a fugitive, he moves across the landscape in search of adventure and intrigue. Feeling certain that the book had chosen me as much as I had chosen it, I made a beeline to the checkout counter.

At my desk, I continued digging through everything I could find on the Organization, searching for a clause, a loophole, my point of entry. In *The Kingdom of the Netherlands Bulletin of Acts, Orders and Decrees* I came across Article 12, which appeared to provide the door. It read: "There is no processing of personal data on the basis of a person's religion or convictions about life, or on the basis of his race, health, or sexual life." I laughed to myself—what else is there? The document then outlined the various jobs within the Organization, including the position 'Head of Service.' Heads of Service are responsible for maintaining the secrecy of sensitive information; protecting the sources from which information is derived; and ensuring the safety of the persons cooperating in the collection of information. Head of Service seemed the appropriate job for me.

On February 10, 2005, the Agency arranged a meeting for the Organization's selection committee to hear what I had to offer. I met them at their building, accompanied by my advisor. Before we could enter, I was searched. The guards took my phone and all other digital devices. I was led to a room with white walls, a mint green carpet, and a large table with no center—an enormous zero.

I proposed that the Organization hire me as its first Head of Service of Personal Data. As Head of Service, I would gather personal data from agents in the Organization as defined by Article 12, beginning with members of the committee. Personal information would be disclosed during private meetings between the agents and myself. These would be conducted at sites of the agents' choosing anywhere in the country, including within the Building. I proposed to write a report based on these encounters, to be publicly available, combining the personal data of the individual agents into a collective file sketching the face of the Organization.

The committee came back with conditions. I could not use agents' real names in my report. They would need aliases. The Organization had two press people, Vincent and Miranda, whose names and faces were publicly known. I would refer to all of my agents as Vincent or Miranda. Every agent I interviewed must have volunteered. The Organization would provide a contact through who all meetings would be arranged. Only my contact would know who the agents were, and only I would know what they said. My report must build a positive image of the Organization's role within society, and provide it with a human face. If my proposal were approved, I would have to be investigated.

I encouraged them to do so.

And so began my vetting. The Organization had hoped to avoid this: Vetting is an expensive and time-consuming procedure but, considering the nature of my proposal, the task was unavoidable. The inspection process was meant to take approximately eight weeks. For the next two months I watched my back.

During that time I did not know what the Organization saw of me or how deeply it explored me. None of my family, friends, or peers told me they'd been questioned. I stopped meeting with anyone who did not endorse or trust the Organization. The weeks passed without incident. I did not sense anyone watching me nor did I see anyone following me. I feared that the Organization did not care, that I was too insignificant, that it did not take me seriously, that it was not vetting me at all.

By mid-March I'd still heard nothing, so on March 17 I called the Committee Head and asked him to meet me the following Sunday at a public art gallery where some of my work was being shown. I hoped that by meeting him alone, without the committee, I could gather inside information on the status of my vetting. I sensed from our preliminary meetings at the Building that he wanted me to pass.

He arrived wearing a suit. We strolled casually through the exhibition until we came to a darkened room in which my videos were being projected. Surveillance footage of Liverpool flashed before us silently. We sat down in the shadows, in two of the black leather chairs I'd selected for the installation. *Hmm.* He leaned back in his seat. *I've been curious to see this footage ever since you showed us those stills in your interview.* The camera pans across a crowd until it finds me, a woman in a red coat, sitting on the edge of a public fountain. It then approaches me slowly—you can feel the controller's hand—until my face fills the screen. The video resolution is low, the contrast high. My skin glows white, my hair and eyes are almost black. I watched the Committee Head meet my pixilated gaze, and basked in the warm tension that our triangle of voyeurism had created. When the scene suddenly cut to an empty street corner, he turned in his chair to look at me.

I confided in him that I'd met with individuals who were opposed to the Organization and was worried about my vetting. He doubted the exchanges would count against me. As for himself, he said, he had stopped paying attention to the conspiracy theorists. *It takes too much time and energy. They treat it like a religion.*

He explained the Organization as a networking system that manages an overflow of information. He drew an imaginary diagram in the air. *Person A is talking to Person B who then talks to Person C.* The Organization has to streamline that data and make it more focused. *We miss a lot of data by filtering it, but it's the only way to make it manageable.*

I told him that the conspiracy theorists I'd met overestimated the Organization, but he said, *No. They are not all wrong. The service processes a lot of information, more than you would imagine.*

A young couple entered the room and he stopped talking. I suggested we leave and get coffee, so we walked across the street to an upscale patisserie. His dark suit and large physique were a funny contrast to its pink decor. He ordered Lady Grey tea and two pastries, one with red and grey striped icing and one with custard. Then he led me to a corner table, hidden away from the rest of the café by the pastry counter.

Once we were settled, he asked about my plans.

Do you plan to return to the States? I could imagine that, after working with the police and now my organization, you might be ready to move on. He lifted his delicate teacup to his mouth; it looked awkward in his grasp.

I replied that it all depended on how my assignment with his organization unfolded—my whereabouts might not matter. I asked if he was familiar with *L'Avventura*, a film by Michelangelo Antonioni that I'd rented the night before; he wasn't. The female protagonist disappears from the screen after the first twenty minutes, never to return, and yet she still remains the protagonist.

I turned to the subject of my vetting, and asked how it was going.

He said the very fact it was being conducted was unprecedented. *Under any other circumstances, my organization would never vet someone like you; you meet none of our criteria.* Nonetheless, he felt confident I'd pass. He explained that vetting would not give me a title but security clearance. As Head of Service I would be entitled to a salary and retirement benefits. *That is not possible.*

I told him I'd need a title.

He grinned. *Perhaps you can be a consultant.*

I asked if he knew of others like me who have been hired by the Organization.

No, he said.

We left the patisserie and strolled along the canal. The sun was setting and the sky was purple. Things felt relaxed between us. He confessed that it would take him a while to understand the way I worked, and it would probably take the other committee members even longer. He asked me to be patient, and promised to offer his advice whenever he could. *We will make this assignment work.*

He said *we.*

Then he added—in a straightforward, typically Dutch manner—that I had a funny way of dressing. *It is half-classic and half, well...* He searched for the word.

I offered strange.

Yes. Your bag, for instance.

I was carrying a small leather purse with a handclasp. I bought it secondhand. I told him I like it because the leather is old and feels soft to the touch. Here, I said. Feel it. I motioned for him to stroke it and he did. Then I asked, Do you always dress so conservatively?

Is this conservative? He seemed insulted.

I tried to recover. Next time we meet you should wear leather pants. He blushed and smiled shyly. Anyway, how a person dresses does not say everything about who he really is.

He looked himself over and said, *This is who I really am.*

Well, I thought, we'll see.

It was almost dark. We kissed one another goodbye and said we'd see each other soon at the Building. I watched him walk away. He waved and turned the corner. I stood where I was, watching the empty street.

I had found my breach.

One week later I received a phone call from the Agency advisor. He casually informed me that the Committee Head was leaving his position and would be replaced by another agent in a different department. This was a terrible setback. I explained the gravity of the decision to my advisor, but he did not understand. Advisors rarely do. Projects such as this cannot be mediated by institutions in an official manner, but must be delicately handled by me personally. I knew this from working with both the Dutch and British police.

Later, as I learned more about the Organization and its policy on "agent loving," I came to wonder if the replacement of the Committee Head was a precautionary step on the the the Organization's part. Agent loving is defined by the Organization as an inappropriate, intimate attachment between agents. An agent from the service typically becomes too close to an agent in the field—a member of the public hired by that agent to gather information. The fear is that the bond between the two will supersede their commitment to the service, leaving it vulnerable. Perhaps the Organization had sensed, as I had, the potential for agent loving between the former Committee Head and myself.

Unaware of the term at the time, and feeling no bond or loyalty to the Organization in the first place, I contacted the now-former Committee Head of my own accord and planned to meet with him again.

The rest of the year passed with little contact from the Organization. I kept busy and continued to work on related projects—I always have a few on the go until one gains momentum and overtakes the rest. Since I did not know if and when

my vetting would go through, I thought it best to stay local.
I rented a workspace in another part of the city, in a former
hospital complex. It was above the old crematorium, with high
ceilings and exposed piping. I hung large drawings and graphs
I'd made on the walls, pinned up my lists of questions for the
Organization as well as their answers, and printed out film
stills that conjured the inside of the Organization as I imagined
it as well as the characters I might find there. I read *Cockpit*
during coffee breaks. The novel is written from the perspective
of Tarden, the protagonist and rogue operative, and organized
into short scenes that follow one another like beads on a string,
without climax or resolution. In each scene, Tarden enters into
someone else's life, altering it irrevocably, for better or for
worse. I read them as proposals. Often on my evening bike rides
home I rented relevant films to watch later that night in bed,
under my pitched roof. I regularly checked in with my advisor
to see if there'd been any progress, but he rarely knew more
than I did. I got into the groove of waiting, which was good. As
I would come to learn, waiting and its source, bureaucracy, are
conditions of working with the service.

It was December 12, 2005, when I finally received my vetting results in the mail. The letter was written in Dutch. The
sparseness of the document signaled to me that I'd failed, or
worse, that I'd been dismissed—perhaps for speaking with the
activists—and taken off the commission. I called my advisor
and nervously recited the Dutch for him to translate. I'd passed.
It was a certificate of non-objection and my security clearance,
vetting number 2485536/01. I had permission to begin.

The Organization's communications department contacted me almost immediately. They asked me to make an infomercial in which I introduced myself to the agents, as I'd need them to volunteer to meet with me and offer their personal data.

That night I met a friend I'll call M, a Dutch designer fifteen years my senior, for drinks at his favorite bar. Meeting him in the evenings had become a habit of late. The bar was close to his house, in a residential area near a retirement home, at the foot of a small and charming bridge no more than a three-minute bike ride from Nieuwmarkt. He knew most of the pub's regulars. Some of the ladies, who beneath their pink lipstick and heavy concealer looked like they'd been through some rough times, flirted with him familiarly. During that period of intense research, talking to M had become akin to sketching. Ideas crackled between us like electricity, taking unpredictable and exciting turns. I inevitably drank and smoked too much with him but he took care of me, often cooking elaborate meals for me after I'd worked too long and too late in my studio. By this point my relationship with my boyfriend was over. He'd moved back into his newly renovated flat, and our place on Spuistraat had become just another canal house I would bike past. M kept my mind sharp and my belly calm. He grounded me in a way that this city, and those I had known here thus far, had never quite managed.

Over white wine and cheese, I told M about the infomercial. Our conversation turned to the film I'd rented the night before, Godard's *Weekend*, and an early scene that had particularly inspired me. In describing it to him, I became so involved in the retelling that I began to reenact it. He sat back against the window with a wineglass in one hand and a cigarette in the other, watching me. When I had finished, he nodded. *That's your video.*

A few days later we hired a friend of his, a Dutch documentary filmmaker, to do the camerawork and made the infomercial at M's house.

I am sitting on a chair with my shirt falling provocatively off my shoulder. I describe the scene in *Weekend* in which the female protagonist tells her story: "He always starts with these really beautiful women—" The screen cuts to the word data on a black background. A dramatic chord of music drowns out my voice, just as happens to the girl in *Weekend*. It cuts back to a close-up of my face. "—and this one is no exception. She is young, beautiful, wearing only her underwear, sitting on a desk." I bring my feet up onto the chair. I am wearing tight-fitting jeans. "The light in the room is dim, tinted orange by curtains closed before the window." M created this effect by laying manila paper over the sliding glass doors. "Behind the desk sits a man. He is in a vest, smoking a cigarette, taking notes." I move my hand as if smoking. "As he listens, she recounts her experience of the night before, engaged in a ménage à trois." In the video, as I had done in the bar, I recount her account.

I sent copies to the communications department and my newly assigned contact at the Organization. My contact said she appreciated the video's elliptical approach but was concerned that many of the agents wouldn't understand its intention. The man at the communications department was one of them. Furthermore, he complained, a six-minute monologue was too long.

I edited it down. I took only a short clip from the last minute of the video. By that point, I have finished my story and am smiling into the camera, waiting for the record light to go off. It doesn't. Confused, I raise my eyes to M's. He is standing above the cameraman, grinning with his arms folded. He nods and I understand what they want: I should stay as I am, staring into the lens. I engage the camera again. In the absence of my voice, I feel exposed and almost laugh. My body temperature rises. I become aware of the cameraman and his lens as a thin and fragile veil. Through it, we hold each other's gaze. When the record light finally dims, we are both sweating.

I sent the one-minute clip to the man in the communications department and this time he distributed it. The video was broadcast throughout the Building on its informational monitors, interspersed between news updates and other feeds to which I did not have access. The communications department added a link at the end, directing agents to an intranet site on the Organization's server that offered further information on my project and how to reach my contact. The original edit was also available there, but it took a few more clicks to reach it.

The video was a success. Agents were drawn in. They called my contact to volunteer and meetings were arranged.

And then it all began. The front door of the Building opened, and a series of its employees filed out. Before the year was through, I had met privately with six different agents. Each time I awaited one, I didn't know who or what to expect. I trusted them to recognize and approach me. At restaurants, bars, airport meeting points, and anonymous rooms within the Building I spoke with them for hours. I listened as the Organization had commanded, without the aid of any recording devices, using only pen, paper, and memory. I compiled a series of notebooks on the agents, always circling back to the subject of the Organization. I used what I learned from one agent and applied it to the next. In these early meetings, I focused less on the Organization and more on their personal lives.

By this time my copy of *Cockpit* had become heavily underlined with several sections starred, most notably page 100, the passage about hummingbirds:

> *I was one of the specially trained groups of agents called "the hummingbirds." The men and women of this group are so valuable that to protect their covers no central file is kept on them and their identities are seldom divulged to other agents.*
>
> *Most hummingbirds remain on assignment as long as they lead active cover lives, usually as high-ranking government officials, military or cultural officials based in foreign countries. Others serve as businessmen, scientists, editors, writers and artists...*
>
> *But I always used to wonder what would happen if a hummingbird vanished, leaving no proof...*

Prologue

On August 25, 2008, a representative from the Dutch embassy in Washington, D.C. traveled to my apartment in Brooklyn, New York to hand deliver the redacted manuscript. I had submitted the draft to the AIVD before completing it. It is reformatted here to fit this edition.

ARTICLE 12

Report for the AIVD on the subject of its face.

Submitted on April 17, 2008 to   for redaction.
TO BE READ ONLY BY THE REDACTOR
EDITING THIS TEXT.

Jill Magid © 2008

This report is dedicated to those in the AIVD who keep its secret warm.

December 9, 2005. Phone Call.
Source:

It's late. I am cleansing my face with a cotton ball and toner when the phone rings. He speaks like he is choking. He says wants to meet tomorrow morning, a time earlier than planned, and take me to breakfast at his hotel. I do not ask why he is staying at one.

He is in front of his computer looking up my train schedule. He maps it out like a math problem, naming each track on which I will arrive, the exact time to switch cars, and which direction to walk once I get there. I will meet him in The Hague as usual, but not at Central Station, at another called Mariahoeve. I repeat it to him and he stutters, *No, Maria, like like like the Catholic*. He will be there waiting.

December 10, 2005. Mariahoeve Station, The Hague.
. 8:45pm.

When I get off the train he is leaning against the wall at the back of the station. I see him and he comes forward. He has none of the stutter or shyness he had on the phone last night. He kisses my cheeks and escorts me to his car. He is wearing the navy blue tie he wore the Sunday we last met. His suit has the same pattern as my pants. As we get into his car I tell him we are wearing the same pants.

He starts up the engine and I point to the stick shift. I don't know how to drive it. He asks if I'd like to, and gets out of the car to switch seats with me. We pull up the seat much farther than it was. I ask where the key is and he says *Oh, sorry* and pulls it from his pocket. He explains the clutch in a hand movement with flat palms. I teach him the word 'clutch' and he shows me *in with the clutch* and *lightly on the brake*. His hands become the pedals and show my feet what to do. We go once then twice around the rotary and then he leads me out of the parking lot. I do OK in second.

At the light I stall three times. I have a silent panic attack but appear to remain calm. I am so focused on which pedal is and which isn't the gas and trying to see through the fog he left on the back windshield to register the fact that I am driving the   to a hotel for a buffet breakfast.

As we walk into the hotel I ask him why he is staying here. He isn't. We go into the buffet room. It's like we are on vacation without the vacation. *It's strange*, he says, *but I like it because of that*. When at hotels, he enjoys an English breakfast.

He chooses a table that is enclosed by a semicircular wall, cocooned away from other people. Once we sit, I don't see anyone else but the waiter, who keeps our coffees full.

He smokes   , a box he ordered from the waiter. He smokes a lot of them. I have two. I wonder if he always smokes or if it's his way of dealing with me digging through his life.

I start with religion.

He rocks in his the chair as he speaks. He holds the
in his hand, down below his waist. I hardly see
him smoke it. The smoke rises in a continual stream, up
behind his body.

We are on our fourth cup of coffee. He's in between
plates of food; I have barely eaten. He knows what he believes, simply and strongly. I am jealous. He has organized
his data.

When he leans forward I lean forward, when he leans
back I lean back. He uses his hands a lot.

I move on to race.

People think in images, he says. *Pictures and images are in-
dicators, and discriminatory by nature. The Government is not
allowed to discriminate when it comes to the rights of civilians.
The penal code describes the rights between people, and between
people and the government. When someone is profiled most times
it's simply bad luck. If, for instance, there were a history of people
with red hair committing terrorist acts, people with red hair
would be profiled. It would be bad luck to have, at that point in
history, a head of red hair.*

He does not use psychology or mental games to con-
dition agents at the Organization. He prompts their behavior by asking questions.

I am doing this with him. I am leaning forward when
he is and back when he does, I smoke two cigarettes to
his ten. I wonder if he is used to doing the same and our
movements are suggestions and the leader has been lost.

*Behavioral Training is about the internalization of behavior
rather than forcing behavior into a set pattern. An adult behav-*

ing in a human way is acting out of choice. It's about trust. He leans forward to ash another cigarette that I have yet to see him smoke.

I move on to sex. He looks at me rigidly. He gets very still and stiff when making eye contact with me without the security of speaking.

According to Article 12, the Organization is not allowed to classify its agents by their personal data. One cannot type "homosexual" into the database and get back a list of names. Many people in his section, under his management, are gay. Most of them tell him. *They don't have to but they do.*

I remind him that I am more interested in knowing him and the Organization intimately than hearing about statistics. He nods. *That is why I like what you do.* He pauses without moving, his eyes unblinking. He admits that he is very good at explaining his thoughts in a logical, coherent manner but when we talk about intimacy he fumbles. He will say this repeatedly.

He tells me that in Holland before the 1970s, *The local authorities kept beautiful charts of their citizens.* He makes a hand gesture of the chart. His drawing in the air conjures an image about the size of a large index card. *These charts were more subjective than statistical. The local authorities would make a chart of each person using his personal data: what church he went to, if at all; if he was married; what he was busy with, etc. To do so is no longer legal.* I ask why it was beautiful. *From the perspective of my organization, it was.*

We move back to religion.

He speaks in sliding scales except when something is black and white to him. Then he simply says, *I don't believe this*. He names the subject and then whether or not he believes in it. I ask him if the Organization has humming-birds, the agents I read about in *Cockpit* who are so deep undercover that even other agents don't know about them. He doesn't believe that it does. *An organization cannot function if parts of it are invisible.*

I press the point. Perhaps sometimes there are no other ways to obtain the information?

It is not, he says, *that we should know what or how everyone is doing what he or she is doing; it is that I do not believe we should* not *know someone is doing it.*

He speaks sincerely, but I trust Kosinski more. Perhaps he is naïve about the hummingbirds. I wonder if he's lying, and move him back to sex.

Oftentimes young professionals who work for the Organization meet their partners within the Building.

. That makes it simple. If an agent is in a relationship with a person outside the system that person has to be vetted.

I ask if that means everyone he dates or is 'with' has to be vetted.

He leans forward completely with his elbow on his knee and says he does not know how many partners I have or how active I am in that way, but agents do not have to have *everyone* they are with vetted. *The relationship has to get serious before the Organization needs to know about it.*

That's funny, I remark, So someone knows you're serious about them when they're asked to be vetted.

Once you work for the Organization, you cannot go on TV or the radio or be publicly vocal about political activities. *If you are someone who likes to take center stage, this is not the job for you—you will feel suffocated. You have to be OK with being in the background.* Sometimes he misses being politically active. He does write reports that are widely read. He straightens his back and looks at me with a sense of pride. He has a passion for writing, structured writing; he is good at putting his thoughts on paper, *Very good at it, actually, better than many people who have PhDs.* He is coherent. He is not good at writing on a personal level— much better in the abstract. He blushes. *I'm a little bit of the scientist or the boring intellectual.*

I ask why he thinks scientists or intellectuals are boring. He ignores me and continues. He is better at analyzing than saying what he feels. He tends to rationalize his feelings. People consider him formal.

His mother was rather feminine. *She loved to care for her children.* His father wanted her to take a greater part in society.

He is leaning in, his cigarette has disappeared, his hands rise to his face to frame it like parentheses.

—he leans towards me and takes the edge of my cardigan sweater between his thumb and forefinger. The seams. *Yes, the seams, she can knit without seams.*

He is almost jealous of her ability to do this. She knits clothes without seams for his newborn niece. *Her skin is very sensitive.*

He leans back into his chair, into his abstractedness, and becomes aware of his watch. It is almost noon. He is late. We have been here for more than three hours. He goes to the bar to pay. As he waits for his change he is already busy pressing numbers into his phone.

I ask if he is driving to the Building. He is and will take me there. I think it's better that he drives.

We get into the car. He seems younger than before. He asks me if I noticed the walking boots in the back. I did. He asks if I like to go walking. I tell him how, as soon as I wake up, I bike to the station and take the train to the beach, and walk through the dunes until it gets dark.

He asks me about my boyfriend. I don't have a boyfriend. He is surprised and claims to have met him. I did have one, but we broke up in May. I ask him whom he met, and he describes him. That was not my boyfriend.

He drives me to the Building and says he will continue

but that he can drop me here. I get out of the car and lean in to kiss him. As I close the car door he says, in case he doesn't see me, to have a good trip. I thank him and tell him he'll see me.

He says, *You know, you really are good at vetting me.*

Thank you, I reply, you are good at being vetted.

I want him as my main character.

Later that day,   at the Building. 1:15-4pm.
Source: Vincent I

I am sitting in
                and asks if he can record us.
He is heterosexual, white, male, one-hundred percent
Dutch. Engages in sex only when in a deep relationship;
                                                      ; his
conviction in life is to do well for the world. He is not religious.   . There is a history of twins in
his family, ending thus far with his uncles.
The Building has an in-house newspaper.

                                                  . It
is confidential, beyond my level of clearance. He tells me
that somebody who works for the Organization submits a
column to the paper that questions the methods and work-
ings of the system. He or she does not use their real name.
It may be a group of people. I cannot decide if this makes the
Organization more open in that it publishes the articles, or
more closed in that the writer's identity remains hidden.

December 12, 2005.   Central Station, Amsterdam.
3:30–6:30pm.
Source: Miranda I

She's young, heterosexual, single, monogamous. Of Dutch
heritage.   . Does not lie, feels no

sense of shame. Adheres strongly to authority. I did not ask which department she is in, but it sounds like she sits at a desk and does clerical work.

She is not religious. I say religion and she replies, *None.* Her family is not religious, either, but her grandmother cleaned a church and her grandfather kept it warm with

coal.   . Neither is
religious. They went to Sunday school, as did she, to learn
the basic values, not to believe in them. *If you learn the basic
values you understand the Dutch—religion is so ingrained here.*
She has read the Bible and the Koran. She likes to study
religion because she likes conflict, of which religion is often
the basis.

As for her health, she is active   . She
enjoys eating. She has tried recreational drugs a few times
but wasn't that interested. She sets herself limits and does
not find it difficult to stay within them.

She developed early. She had first boyfriend when she
was fourteen. He was nineteen. *It was a long relationship—
three months.* She worries I might think that she was sleeping around then, but she wasn't. She made a rule: She had
to be with a guy for six months before having sex with him.
Since then she's had three lovers, the first when she was
nineteen. She makes rules with no logic behind them—
the six-month rule fell short. She is currently single and
doesn't date internally at the Organization.

She calls herself a stress smoker, but claims to rarely get
stressed (I notice a pack of Marlboro Reds in her purse). *I
know what I can manage and I don't take on more than that.*
She has no issues of guilt or shame. *I have never done anything of which I am ashamed.*

Her parents are still together. Her father is
. *He communicates well with babies and small animals.*

. She respects his

authority. *Boundaries are important.* Her morals come from her parents and her understanding of the law comes from the police.

As part of the Organization, she feels assured that she is making the world a better place. By better she means, *Safer from physical harm.* She does not want to protect an ideology, only national security.

She is curious *about the inside* of the service; she wants to be in the mix. I cannot picture it—she seems too innocent. *It's hard to keep secrets.* She wants to share everything when in an intimate relationship, but her job makes that impossible. She hopes this does not change her.

I cannot imagine her changing.

December 13, 2005. The Building. 1pm.
Source: Vincent II

I approach the Building.

. My source comes through and greets me. He leads me to his car in the Building's lot. He says that he will be taking me to the mall for lunch.

He is white, male, heterosexual, Dutch. Both his parents

were Protestant. He is superstitious. He believes death is announced by objects breaking spontaneously—a gemstone,
for example, or a ring,

                                          . *There
is fate and predestination, and sometimes there are signs.* The
soul of one is reborn in another. *A lost mother becomes a new
daughter.* He takes a sign and makes a symbol.

                              , *Like a girl sitting
opposite you on the train.* He   is
currently single. As for his marriage of fifteen years, he
refuses to talk about it.

                                          . He
chooses sports that he can do at his own speed when he is
ready.   . He smokes
Reds; they do not give him the same head rush and dizzi-
ness they give me. *Cigarettes are like licorice drops or chocolate:
Once you start you keep going, all the way to three packs a day.*
With some work and self-control this has gone down to
one pack a day. *Eventually it will be one a day and then none—
but not yet.* His team in the Organization is loud; they like
to joke around. *When you don't laugh at least once a day you
lose a day. A day can sometimes include crying.* They listen to
the radio while they work. *Music is an emotion. Music is who
I am.*   . He believes in love
at first sight. It is entirely possible that when he's on the
train tonight after work a woman will sit down across from
him and they will have a connection. She does not have to
be a physical beauty. *Physical beauty fades. What is between
her ears is what's important, that she will be a friend,* the kind
of friend he illustrates by interlocking his fingers together.

Her age doesn't matter. She may be sixty years old. But he is a man, *Of course.* He loves a beautiful body, but he won't be found with a pack of men, hanging over a balcony, leering as women walk by. As for his divorce, *Do you understand?* He does not want to talk about it. He is not ambitious. *You are good at what you are good at; you should strive to get to the position that fits you.* He suits his job well so, for the time being, he will stick where he is. He finds secrets intriguing. *That's why I like my job.*

. He sees the problem and constructs a strategy. It is a creative process, *Which is good, because I am a creative person.* He finds arrogance intolerable. Whether you are on a lower rung or the head of the Organization, you address one another by first name only. *This is a family.* If his team in Holland can prevent a bomb from going off   he believes he's done his job. As for his divorce he repeats with sudden force that he does not want to talk about it.

My brief was that he was an old-timer and conservative in appearance. He was neither.

Later that day.   the bar. 5pm.
Source: Miranda II

Married   heterosexual, sees belief as a crutch, cynical about people, hates sport but does it to be healthy,

                    . Interests include comic books

. No children.

We meet at the hotel bar in The Hague, and sit by the window overlooking the parking lot. Very few people are here. She looks like the incarnation of the reclining nude in Modigliani's painting of 1917—lying on her back atop a red blanket, arms folded up, her hands behind her head which rests on a white pillow. Her lips are heart-shaped, full, and painted dark.   . She is the kind of woman who effortlessly looks dressed up, put together perfectly, even in sweatpants—though I doubt she ever wears them.

The hotel lounge suits her appearance. It is red and lush. The candle on the table is red. The seats are scarlet and deep—they absorb us into their cushions. It's the kind of bar at which you have a 5 o'clock drink before going upstairs to have sex with your boss, both of you in business suits. It looks nice on the surface but you can imagine something else going on here—a hotel bar seems seedy somehow.

She whispers a lot. *You never know who is listening*

. She never thought she would work for the Organization. Someone recommended her and she was approached. She had a quality the Organization wanted; I do not know what it is, and wonder if I have it.

. It is necessary to imagine beyond what can be seen, to sense more than can be heard. The goal is to gather the pieces and choose which direction to follow. It's a big job, mostly done alone. Connections exist that might not appear on first sight but need to be made. *The story evolves through them.* Then you need the facts to ensure the story's not invented. *With the facts you build the story.* The Organization is essentially a giant storyteller. *It runs like a machine. Each agent is a cog in the machine, a frame of the story.*

It's a shame when her friends discuss the news and she knows the whole story but cannot share it. She has to have a thick skin and not feel personally compromised. The media fashions an image, and the public discusses what it's given. she works with lawyers often. Everything has to go through them. She has to explain things as efficiently as possible to ensure they check out legally.

When she gets emotional, the lawyers remain rational. They keep her chained, *Like a dog on a leash*.

Most of the agents have similar worldviews, what is good and what is bad. They have an urge to actively help and protect society. *There are no James Bonds, but there is a strong sense of responsibility. Nobody on the outside is thankful.* Nobody acknowledges when they are doing good work. Discretion is a large part of the job, to go behind the mirror and to see things not as they look but as they *are*.

Before working for the Organization she had time to think about things like the meaning of life and death, but not anymore. A sense of humor is a big part of the job. Some people call it cynicism. *Nothing is holy*.

Ideology can drive people crazy. She has seen a lot of extreme behavior. The Organization's "clients" are not normal. *The majority of the world is not normal.* She can see, from a distance how people think and how they act because of their beliefs. She understands how fanaticism evolves and, when she has the whole story laid out in front of her, can see how ridiculous it looks.

She wishes she could freeze-frame certain moments. She'd ask people to come look at the story from where she is. She wishes she could pull the character out of the story and ask him to look at the bigger picture.

Belief is a structure.

I ask her if she believes in anything, if belief is only that.

.

If she could give a real person super powers, she would make him very strong. He would be able to see into the future, become invisible, and intuitively identify the bad guys. *Bad people would have red noses.* Looking at anyone, he'd be able to see whether they had a red nose. Her super hero would be charming, too. He'd be discreet and efficient. He'd be able to see what a person was going to do. Her hero can freeze time. He would see the opportunities, he'd see the larger picture, he would see change and he would see the bad people. He would banish them to other planets. He would be a he. *Men are less emotional.*

The Organization is not looking for easily stressed people. *They're not good for the work environment or for morale.* It needs people who can deal with unpleasant things in a pleasant way with a positive point of view.

The Organization is family-like. *It is not about sex.* She is attracted to men with strong personalities. She likes the ones who aren't loved by everybody, the ones who are difficult. The attraction is often mutual. She enjoys the challenge, the friction. She does not want a pushover. She prefers not to manipulate but tends to if she can. Her father used to say she was a mean little girl.

I close my notebook and ask her if those were the kind of questions she had expected. *More or less,* she says—she knows the article's criteria, but says she could have taken more. *Remember where I work. Don't forget what my job is. I am used to much worse. In my line of work, the stakes are higher. The consequences are greater. If I were in your shoes, I would take your assignment to the edge. I would push it until we said stop.*

I ask her to teach me how to do so.

I can't give you advice. This is your story. You formulated the questions. Your questions are a mirror to your interpretations of what I say. Your inquiries were broad, so there was a lot of room.

Reflections. One hour later. 10pm.

I am on the train back to Amsterdam after the meeting with Miranda II, exhausted, frustrated, and scribbling in my notebook:

I need to be trained how to interrogate. I want them to tell me details. "*Love means being able to be yourself*" means nothing. I cannot write that under the Article's category Sexual Life. I need to approach the assignment differently. When I ask about their health I should ask about their toenails, their ankles, the hair on the backs of their calves, visit each part of their bodies like   tells me to over the phone when I have insomnia: "*Start from your toes and slowly move up your legs, concentrate, relax, be aware of each muscle*". Interrogate the composition of their every cell. When the agent says   I need to know everything

                              how he studies to improve. How exactly he interprets the word religion. Otherwise I learn facts about them, but not how they *feel*, who they truly are, or, most

70

importantly, how they do their jobs. I cannot penetrate the Organization if I cannot get through to its agents. Like the spider in the web, I need a strategy. I want to know their methods, whether they brief a person before they interrogate him, if he knows what he will be asked. And if so, does that prepare him to speak or prepare him to hide? I need to be trained. I know nothing.

I want to have dinner waiting for me at home. I call . It's late but he says, *Come over.*

What was I thinking getting myself into this?

He laughs. *Yes, what were you thinking?*

It is too much, I say, to interview two agents in one day. And I am doing it all wrong.

He is silent.

I am doing it wrong,   I messed it all up.

Come, he says, *I will make you something warm.*

          is in the kitchen; I am lying on the sheepskin rug near the stereo, watching him cook.

I think the morning source left upset with me, I tell him. I said to him, I hope I didn't overwhelm you, and he said, "*Well, you did,*" with a smile, but the kind of smile that will change. He will review what he said and be upset. I think he was my only successful interview. I think I need to keep going until they say stop, keep pushing until the border is drawn, until I hear, *That is too far.* Otherwise I have not gone far enough. He was the only one who laid down the line. "*I will not talk about that,*" he said. He defined a border.

          keeps making the soup and watching the mushrooms. He listens in such a way that I can hear him listening.

My questions, I continue, were too broad. I thought that would give them room. I wanted to use what I learned from the cognitive interview—do not lead the witness, do not close off memory, let them speak and they will recall more—but this does not apply as a general method, not without a specific incident. When the questions are open I get, "*Love means being able to be yourself*"; "*we are like a family*"; "*I want to do good for the world.*" Zero. I get nothing.

carries two bowls of steaming soup to the work-table and moves his computer aside. I get off the rug and join him. He fills my glass with wine.

I don't want to push too hard,   but if I am going to get past the surface, I might have to.

Give it time, he says, and passes me the salt. *They chose you for a reason. You'll learn what you need to do.*

December 19, 2005. Café   , Amsterdam. 10:30am.
Contact meeting.

At my request, my contact meets me at a bar. I ask her to teach me how to interview, how to be   ,
how to get to the source faster, deeper, smoother, so the cut is invisible and the insertion deep.

She laughs in response. *There is nothing we can teach you. You are already getting far more than we expected. One source told me that she admitted to you how and when she lost her virginity. Not even her best friend knows that.*

I tell her I'd discovered something. After asking questions, I put down my pen and close my notebook. The air changes; our roles dissolve; we critique ourselves openly, as our own audience.

She confirms, *That is what we do too.*

But I am not permitted to record them, so I have to.

Don't worry, she says, *You are getting a lot.*

She needs to talk to me about another issue. I know what it is. The source from yesterday afternoon was upset. I upset him.

Yes, you did. He felt you got very personal.

My title is Personal Data Consultant.

Yes, but he did not realize what you meant by personal. Maybe that is my fault. Perhaps I need to brief them better. He said to her, "She asked me about religion!" Yes... and? "She asked me about my divorce, and when I said I did not want to talk about it, she said OK. But then she worked her way back to it and asked me again!"

Yes, I did this. It was the only time he began to break into some kind of real and thoughtful space. I tell her I am looking for the real story, not the niceties that come with a toasted cheese sandwich.

She tries to explain my position in relation to the Organization. I thought I understood. I didn't. "*Operational*" *means going out and collecting data. You are operational. A person on the outside who agrees to give information is called a "source". A source is protected. The term for this is* Bron Besherming, *meaning Source Protection. Anyone who works for us will understand* Bron Besherming.

From now on, she will tell them to consider themselves sources rather than volunteers. As a source, they will not talk about being one. Nor will they speak about talking to me. This is necessary. The morning source—   — is not acting like a source but like a messenger, an internal alarm, and, as my contact confirms, he can be successful. *He has a big mouth and knows everybody.*

I tell her that while Vincent II said I went too far Miranda II said I did not go far enough. I do not think I pushed it.

Yes, she says, the source told her as much.

I did not reach her boundaries.

No, she confirms, *You did not.*

Miranda II said, at the pen-down-close-the-notebook moment, that if she were me, she would take them to the edge.

Of course she would say that, says my contact.

. *Her job is to go too far.*

From now on, I tell her, this is what I need to happen: Before I meet a source, I want to be briefed. I want to know the source's job within the Organization, if they are operational, how they collect and process information. I want to get at least what they expect from their own sources.

For the good of my assignment, she gives me permission. From now on, I will know which department they work in.

She explains the seven departments in the Building. *They're called 'directions.'*

.

I should know, she assures me, that she and the Committee Head are on my side, even more now than before.

They realize that, in researching my assignment, events like the one with Victor II will happen. They are prepared to protect me and defend my methods. Their job is to support my role so that I can write my report and find the face of the Organization. When I suggest talking on a more banal level, asking instead about their morning routine—how they get dressed, what they're wearing now, how they make breakfast—she rejects it. *You are operational and your target data is not that kind of data. Keep going the way you are.*

She says not to worry about   . *In a way it's a good thing. He will funnel the sources—those who have not been scared off will come forward.* But this is problematic. I want the tunnel vision people, too.

I tell her that I learned the Organization does not hire people who believe in God.

She falls back in her chair, amazed. *But we do!*

Well, I say, my sources thus far do not.

How funny, in the past there was a very large religious constituent. It was central to the Organization.

I need people from this group.

Yes, you do, she says. *I will get you people who believe in God.*

December 19, 2005. Café   , Amsterdam.
Source: Vincent III

We meet in Amsterdam   8pm. I am sitting at the bar when he enters. He registers me slowly. We go up the stairs and sit down at a table on the second floor beside a stained glass window. He orders a beer. I order wine.

Let's start easy, I say, with religion.

Religion? Religion is not easy.

OK. We'll come back to religion. Let's talk about race. He points to his face: *White.*

But he doesn't look white. So I ask, What is your background? Where are your parents from?

Oh, so that's what you mean by race.

The Organization is not about hierarchies. It is flat.

Who?

But how do they know of me?

Will this show up on my passport at the airport?
No, I don't think so.

Working for the Organization brings him excitement but only when he contemplates it, which he doesn't often do. People get used to everything.

Sometimes when he is watching TV he sees the Building. He cannot imagine how these broadcasts make sense to anyone who doesn't work within it. He knows so much about these topics he has to try to rid himself of all that baggage in order to understand how the general public might see it. *For so many people what happens must seem so mysterious, even though there is so much information out there.*

I ask him whether hummingbirds exist in the Organization.

.

When people are hired, they are told they are easing into a warm bath. *They actually tell you this!* My source has heard them say it. *But they neglect to finish the sentence: It is like a warm bath, but you can get burned.*

It takes a while to get to know the Organization, especially to understand the people who have been there the longest. *The elders know how to charm, they will smile and make you feel welcome, but they know what they want and they know how to get it. They are rats.* He supposes, then, that he is also a rat and shrugs because, by his estimation, he is not as skilled. *The really good ones know how to put on a nice face and get exactly what they want. You gotta respect that.*

I do.

The new hires think everyone is nice. *On a superficial level we are all one big family, but there is an ocean underneath the surface. You have to be very smart to get ahead.* It took him two years to wise up. He was too open, said more than he should have, aired his own opinions too often, didn't know when to close his mouth or to whom he should—and shouldn't—speak. Even now he is still not a star player.

He has always been nosy.

.

He was quite a good student in high school—*The best in history class*. He likes to know why things happen, why people do the things they do, who influences whom, why people in other countries react as they do. He used to read the newspapers every day. Now, with this job, he gets a glimpse beyond the headlines. *It is satisfying to be someone who isn't fooled by the press.* He is no longer part of uninformed society. When he reads history books now, he perceives more than is given, more than what is written. He can pick up the text and look beneath it.

Lots of people can put a civilized face on for the outside world and hide the evil one within. Society allows us to show only one face. Society encourages us to hide. Look at Amsterdam, for example, at the guys who go to the Red Light District. Eighty percent of them are nice guys and husbands. But I don't think those guys are evil; it is too simplistic to define evil. The world is more complicated than that.

It is difficult for me to believe, he says, *that anyone is one hundred percent evil. I am not naïve, but my basic thinking is that you should trust someone until they break it. I try to remember this because the moment I lose that I become a cynical secret agent.*
So, I ask, are secret agents typically cynical?
No, on the contrary. An agent must be open to everything.

Now he is part of history, he can influence it, perhaps only in the Netherlands but, still, he can make a difference. He likes to believe that maybe, now, he can change history.
He reads a lot about Islam. *It is very beautiful. If you are Islamic you have to demonstrate your faith; it's not enough to just believe. It's a pity that Islam is being cast in such a negative way. The Koran states it is impossible that Jesus was the Son of God.*

There is only one god—you cannot split him. The Catholics split him in three. I like to keep him whole. Man cannot be half a god. It is impossible for me to accept that one man can be higher than another man. A prophet is different from a god.

For many people who work at the Organization, it is their lifeblood. For him, it is his job. He sees it as a choice. *What is important is the way of living. Just defend the country and our democracy, and that is it. That is our way of life.*

Working in intelligence is like playing chess with information. *I play chess with colleagues in other fields and other countries. My information is my pawn but, on the next level, the pawn is the intelligence officer. It's like a spider in the web, and the web keeps getting bigger. You have to know who you are playing with and who is playing with you.*

Who is on top?

No one. There are lots of chess games going on at the same time, with different games stacked on top of one another. The politicians' role is especially interesting.

He doubts God wants to be a chess player—*If he exists. You know, he might be an evil God. Is that blasphemy? What does God want? Perhaps he started off with a good idea and made a little world, but it got too big and he lost his grip. Perhaps he's made a nice place for himself in heaven. Perhaps the world is too complicated even for God.*

When I shut my book he says, *I have a question for you. Whenever you asked me a question and I responded you would say you felt the same and then give me an example. Were you telling the truth or are you just really good at this? Do you do this with everyone or do you, in fact, truly identify with me?*

With this question, the energy at the table spikes. I

answer carefully. I know that it is both: a tactic to match him, and a sense of when to give back because he has given a lot. In describing my own experiences in a detailed way, I am providing an example of how I want him to speak. I give detail so that I get detail. I guess this is what happens when you ask for information from a man who is trained to get information.

You should come and work for us.

Interlude. December 20, 2005.

I get a call from my contact informing me that Vincent III feels I did not go all the way with him last night. He believes I can go farther and wants to meet me again. I agree. She plans for us to meet again on the 26th.

December 26, 2005. The Building,   .
Source: Vincent III. Second meeting.

It is the first time I have taken the train to the Building rather than the bus. When I get out I am disoriented. The streets are dim and empty. The Dutch celebrate two days of Christmas; today is the second.

The Building looks deserted, so dark as to be invisible.

I come out of the bathroom and turn towards
. Through the doorway I can see two plastic coffee cups
sitting on the table. The source comes up behind me, I am
unsure from where. He says that we can sit in the room he
reserved or here on the comfortable lounge chairs. I prefer
the meeting room with a table for my notes.

He is the officer on duty today, 10am to 10pm. He jokes
that today he is the most protected man in Holland:

After ten minutes, there is a pause. I say, OK, I am here
for you. You said that I did not hit your boundaries, which
means you know what those boundaries are and also that
you know what you want to tell me.

Oh. Well, that makes it easy for you.

I ignore him and repeat: What do you want to tell me?
He saw an ad for his job in the paper
     . He fit the requirements well. He did not realize
what it would entail. For the first two years he treated
the job as he treats grant applications. He would propose
what he wanted to investigate, they would say OK, and
that's what he did. He figured that, *In a way, it was all just
a load of bullshit. If you wrote it well they paid you for it, just
like a grant.*

He was slow to realize that this was not the way to do
it. This attitude did not position him where he wanted to
be. It took him two years to understand. *Too long.* Then a
job came up he really wanted and everyone in the Building
said he was perfect for it. He applied twice and did not get
it. He did not apply a third time but they put him on the
list anyway, and he still did not get it. It was the first time
he did not get what he wanted. He realized he was not
in control.

An agent handler finds people from the public, called
agents in the field, and pays them to work for him. It is a
person on the inside who finds a source on the outside to
get him information. *You are in control because you are out on
the streets*, he says, *You have to go to the Building, but not much.
You find the right person and you say something like, 'Hey, we
know a lot about you, I work for them,—do you want to work for
me?' If I were trying to hire you,* he says to me, *because, say, you
are friends with terrorists,*

                                             ?'

It's like your job, he says. *You build up trust with people in order to get information.*

Do you tell them who you are?

We are obliged to. (I'm unsure if that means yes).

He is surprised. *Everyone wants to feel important, like you want to be his friend. And you act like you* are *a friend, but you're not. You just want information.*

I don't think that job sounds so difficult.

Really, he says? *Don't forget, you have to get them to betray. It is difficult work.*

I would like that job—not the betrayal part, but the part about being a spy in the field.

You'd be good at it.

I tell him I want the Organization to hire me.

We can't, you are American.

But don't you need some information in New York? Kosinski writes that in his service many hummingbirds were famous artists, especially film directors.

He nods. *They have the perfect cover. They travel, they spend time with all different kinds of people—even shady ones. Maybe your guys will hire you.*

No way, the Americans are untouchable. I have been to the embassy and they are not interested in who I am or what I do.

He smiles slyly and says, *Don't be so sure.*

I would rather work for them. Somehow the betrayal seems less offensive, as if, in a foreign country, my actions do not count.

I say, I already work for your organization. I have security clearance.

You know, I think you are the first non-Dutch person to have that. You are the first non-Dutch person to sit across from us and talk with us one-on-one like this.

I ask how an agent handler entering the field finds his targets.

We have our ways, but I cannot tell you. You know we work in secret. It is not something you advertise in the paper. We start laughing. *You're not going to see in the paper, 'Man needed to fly plane into skyscraper, call this number.' It's a play. It's a political play.*

Are there more male than female agents in the field?

It's not about gender—it's about character. He thinks women are actually better suited to the job. *They are more sensitive to feelings, they have a deeper sympathy for relation-ships.*

He suspects they wanted him all along for the job he has now. *It's a similar role, but on the inside.* Instead of relat-ing to the guy on the street he relates to agents in other services, the professionals. He negotiates with them. If he stays a few years longer he knows they will send him to cool places, like Pakistan—

A few *years?*

He nods and continues.

His friends say he is striving for something that does not exist. No one is one hundred percent in control of his life.

I ask him if he cheats on his girlfriend for the physical pleasure or to assert his freedom.

For the freedom. I do it when I need to know I still have control, to prove to myself I am still free.

He tells me that to work for the Organization you must be interested in everything that happens. You must be nosy. You must also behave like the perfect person so there is no possibility of blackmail. An older colleague told him when he first joined, *"If you are going to be with a woman and cheat at least cheat with someone on the inside."*

One time he was in   at the same time as another agent who didn't know he was there—

So you were a hummingbird!

No, he shakes his head,

.

December 27, 2005.   .
Contact meeting.

Due to sudden changes in my personal life, I will be relocating to New York City in a week, after living in Holland for five years. I call my contact to tell her. We schedule a meeting in Amsterdam, at   (the bar at which I met   ), at 5:30pm. We arrive at the same moment and sit down close to one another at the round corner table on the ground floor. She is wearing jeans, a green T-shirt with a thin lace collar like pajamas, and a hooded sweatshirt. She does not look well. I ask her why.

She tells me she had not picked up her phone when I called her the day before because she'd broken up with her boyfriend,   . I knew the story. They'd been together for six months, which also meant that I'd known her for over seven. She says she's never cried as much as she has in these last two months. *Either the relationship—or I—was going to break.* She told him as much on the second day of Christmas, the night I met Vincent III at the Building. He said he knew he had done this to himself, and that he understood her decision. He told her she was the perfect woman for him but that he was completely unwilling to change his life to fit hers.

I recognize this.

She said, *The last time he broke plans, something in me broke.*

I recognize this too.

            —the one she takes at night, after finishing work at the Building—reviewed her last night. They spared nothing. *Then again, that's their job.* The class is quite serious.

I can imagine this.

. She agrees. They are trying to break her.

I explain what I began on the phone, that I am leaving the country, possibly for good. From this point on I will need to travel across the ocean to meet with my sources. She is disappointed, having enjoyed our frequent meetings. She says she had just begun to know me, and now I am leaving.

I ask her if she thinks the Organization would consider hiring me to spy for them in the United States. She tells me it's unlikely.

2006. New York.

When in Holland I look for the face of the Organization. In New York, I begin to look for mine. I read about the CIA daily in the papers as a phone-tapping scandal heats up. I observe the policemen at work around the city. I become close to one, and persuade him to train me off the record. I apply to private investigators for work. I seek to be trained, in any way I can.

My contact and I speak regularly between my visits to Holland, and I review my notebooks often. I realize that the more directly I had approached my sources, the more elusive the Organization had been. I replay the conversations with my sources in my mind: There was always a barrier. I cannot discern the boundaries the Organization has given me, but I can sense they've been defined. Someone has drawn a line. There must be a way around it that will lead me into the center, to the face of the Organization.

I study *Cockpit* now as a guide to a kind of organization I have yet to see. In Holland, I am looking to reveal Kosinski's world, the kind of service that he describes, where the hummingbirds pull all the strings and know all the truths. Someone inside the Organization must know about the hummingbirds. Someone knows the whole story, beyond mere fragments. Someone knows who I am and where I fit in. I grow more determined. To find the face at the center I will become a hummingbird and I will use the Organization to learn how to be one, because I believe it does this, it can do this, it is doing it all the time.

February 16, 2006.

The Buildings Agency advisor sends me a message in New York. I will be reviewed upon my next trip to Holland. In preparation for the Agency's assessment,

Two days later I land at Schipol airport and take the train to   's house. Over lunch with   , I receive a phone call from my contact.

90

. This is for my sources' protection. Nobody, not even she, can know what transpires between us.

.

She calls me back a few hours later with the schedule of my appointments.

February 18, 2006.   , Amsterdam. 3-7:30pm.
Source: Vincent V

It's Saturday. The café is popular.
                              . I wait near the bar, unsure of where to stand. Finally, a man approaches me from the crowd. *Are you Jill?*
                    . I doubt he is much older than I am. He tells me that he has been standing close by for some time but did not identify me. He thought he saw me earlier, but it was another woman in a red coat.

We sit down at a table in the service section and wait
for the waitress to come.

. He
looks like he was a jock or frat boy in prep school. He has
that clean-shaven, all-American look that Tommy Hilfiger
advertises. Photograph him in a crisp white tennis suit and
the gay boys will smile.

Once we are settled and drinks have been ordered, he
tells me that he is organized. *I have prepared what I want to
say to you.* I explain that our conversation is not going to
work like that. If that were the way it worked, I tell him,
you could have written me an essay and dropped it in the
mail. We are here, together, now. Let's be present, or nothing real can happen.

He turns red, and I tell him so.

*I am very careful when it comes to talking about what I
do*, he explains. *. Generally, I do not mention it to people at all.
And when people I ask, I prime my reactions.*

.

I ask about his accent.

?

Exactly. You sound like me.

He smiles—or does he gloat?

. I can imagine him in a baseball cap.

His job is somewhat removed.

. *There is nothing personal about it.*
. *There are no targets.* He determines
what is important. He tells the spider in the web what to
listen to. *I put the fly in his web.* An agent handler directs
the agent in the field on what to do, what information to
obtain. He's the next guy in, the one who receives the information. He has nothing to do with how the information
is obtained, but outlines what is still needed.

I ask him if he knows how information gets to him,
even if it is not his job to do so.

There are a few ways. He uses the bar as an example.
He could go up to the waitress and just talk to her. *That
is a sneaky way of getting information.* He could be forthright or underhand—he might stress how much he needs
her help. He is fascinated by a capacity to play into what
drives people. *People do things in order to find meaning in
life. People want to have relevance. People focus on their own
situation—they want to talk about their own lives. You can use
this.* He could get a job here. He could have someone else
get a job here. He could train someone for the role. *Then
I'd be working as an agent handler, and that someone would be
my spy.* That way, he reduces his own risk.

This job requires dealing with more than most people

do but, from the look of it, it's just an average job. The daily routine seems pretty normal   . It's like he lives inside another envelope, and no one in the city can talk about what he does. He exists in two worlds but is aware of this. *I am not schizophrenic. I would be schizophrenic if I was not aware of this.*

He says he's been thinking about the ritual of his job. *It's almost a religious experience, to enter the gate into the Building. You are accepted. The gate keeps others out but it reminds us that we are on the inside.*

You were at the Building over Christmas?
Yes.
Why were you there?
I am not going to tell you.

I can see that this bothers him. His boyish grin disappears. He looks at me differently, perhaps with more respect, or at least with greater interest.

He tells me a story. *There was this one target.* They knew everything about him: his private life, his wife, his lover. One of the team members was in the checkout line at the supermarket. A man nearby began to speak, and he froze. He recognized the target's voice. *It is amazing to know someone so intimately and yet not know them at all.*

                    . Bivangst *means 'the catch of the day.'* He does not think he could handle it, though. *I*

would have trouble getting that close. He would not want to
know who the target really was, as an individual. *I wouldn't
want to see it slip.* They might be watching the target,

               *. And I might have to think, what if he's a
good guy? He may have shot three people but what if—*
Is it ever OK to kill?
He turns red. *You are persuasive.*

   .

*We prevent attacks. We make a point. We are responsible
both to individuals and to the government; we respond to those
who threaten the nation.* He speaks with a gentle authority,
not with condescension but like a very well trained student
that has great respect for his subject.
    It becomes complicated when you get too close to a real person.

               . But I don't deal with personal lives.
I want to know about your personal life. It's my job.
My personal life in relation to the job?
Not necessarily.
He turns red.

He responded to an ad in the paper for the Organization.
He was intrigued by the idea of working at a place like that.
He arrived for his interview by car. *I was nervous they would
take down my license plate and know everything about me.*
    He tells me that I am entering the Organization in a time

of generational change. The general public used to support what it did. Everything's changing now. The Organization is not static or predictable like it was twenty years ago. *Look at society. It's communicating differently. There is deep mistrust. We have to be flexible. We are a reflection of society so we had better bend when it bends. There might be space for you within the Organization because of this. We need to translate, not just transmit.*

He feels he is unable to be fully creative in his job. His authority rests in terms of judgment. He makes the call as to whether it is worth investing resources in monitoring someone. He dictates what he wants, and what he needs. He has to think of original ways of approaching people. And then there is the long process of documenting his work. *It is so slow.* Everything must be retrievable.

In his free time he likes to look at art. He looks at me and grins.

. *Patterns and movement. I think there is a strong connection between pattern, movement, and everyday life.* He likes to look at the bicycle barge—a four-story parking garage for bicycles—outside the central station. *I know it's because of a lack of space, but it's so absurd. Maybe that is because we know a structure like that is designed for cars.*

He takes care of himself physically and spiritually.

. *I believe in the ephemeral.* Things happen for a reason

. Even so, he finds experience difficult without judgment.

                              . I wondered if he was married.

               . He says this with conviction, like it's a goal. I wonder if he has begun to regard our talk as a kind of date.

Working for the Organization puts him in a position of power. *It's a kind of arrogance.*   . He cannot imagine power without secrecy.

The job is about observation. *There are moral issues attached to that.* It is not a choice of life or death. *Choices are incidental. The question is: how far will you go?* You must delve into a person's life. *Are the results of this kind of secret probing substantial enough to validate the method? It's easy to justify it from the security of an organization.* Employees are supposed to take a neutral position.

Working in special operations affects its employees' personal relationships. You have to believe that the sacrifices you are making are worth it. Some people are really good at special operations. It can be addictive. *Some people have an innate talent at transforming themselves.*

The waitress asks if we need more drinks. I've already had three cups of tea. He looks at his watch and is surprised by the time. It is 7:30pm. My stomach groans. My head feels light from talking. We get the check, stand up, and put on our coats. He seemed much bigger at the bar. Outside, he turns to face me. He says that, even after talking for four-and-a-half hours, he regrets our meeting's over. *I feel as if we are leaving in the middle.*

I advise him to call my contact if he has more to say and wants to meet again.

Interlude. February 20, 2006. Meeting with my contact and Committee Head,   Café in The Hague.

It is the day of my review. I wait for my contact outside a Bruna, a magazine chain store in The Hague Central Station. The Committee Head joins us outside. We cross the tram tracks to   a seedy coffee shop with a pinball machine by the door. Following their lead, I order an espresso and an amaretto with whipped cream on the side.

.

.

I discuss, in general terms, how the meetings with my sources have developed and why I believe I should now be trained. To truly understand the Organization, I need to be a part of it rather than on the outside looking in.

. And did you know the Director

wants to meet you?

Why does he want to meet me?

He saw your video on the intranet site and is curious—and he is the director. Sources asked to volunteer for an assignment.

How is he curious?

She chuckles. *We will see. I need to know when you can meet him. He is the one who will decide whether you should be trained.* She thinks it might be a good idea, but is unsure how the director will react. My contact, who is always trying to help, suggests that I could apprentice for someone. I concur and try to persuade the Committee Head. I remind her of their built-in system of protection: they can white-out anything I write. Maybe, I tell them, everything will be whited-out in the end. I might come out of this saying nothing.

.

I openly discuss my interest in

and my fascination with anonymity: how sources were often well-known writers or public figures; how one of my sources was the editor of a political magazine and can never again write from the same position. I cannot imagine giving up my authorship if I worked for the Organization, never again having anything I wrote or made accredited to me—unless, of course, I was a hummingbird and my public career was my front.

My contact replies, *Well then, you had better never publish your work about the Organization under your own name.*

As she says this, I realize it's a good idea. It makes me shake and feel scared, the sensation I get when I know something is right but will be difficult to do.

I give them dates of when I can meet with the director.

We talk about the people I have met, how some came with an agenda that I had to make them drop.

Repeating my interest in
                                     I confide that my fear—unlike my source who didn't want to become too personally invested in a target's narrative—is that I might actually be able to do this job. I am drawn to it. They share a look and a smile. The Committee Head says, as my contact nods, *Yes, you could do it. And you would be good at it.*

We leave   for the Government Buildings Agency. My review panel includes the Agency Representative, his superiors—including the Director—my contact, and my Committee Head. As instructed, I share nothing of my files. I give the Agency an estimated timeline for the rest of my assignment and a dummy book with a hummingbird on the cover that   designed. My contact and Committee Head explain to the Representative and his colleagues that any disclosure of my writings would be a security breach and a betrayal of my sources.

.

February 20, 2006.
Source: Miranda III

        . Her neighborhood looks like a gated community or a retirement home in New Jersey, with short houses that sink uncomfortably into the ground. Every house seems to have a cat in the window or a colored flag coming off the front door representing nothing other than itself, like the houses in a beach town. She waves from the window as we drive up. I thought she was going to be the woman from the committee, the young cute one that sits next to my contact, but she is older   . I have to readjust how I thought the next few hours were going to be.

Before I get out of the car my contact gives me the brief. The source has been with the Organization for a long time,

                        she is a nice, pleasant woman. I realize that nearly all her briefs include this last sentence, and I begin to resent it.

The source invites me in. She wears a white cotton turtleneck and bright pink slippers that leave much of her pink feet visible. We go into the living room. I sit down on one of the two couches; she sits on the other. There is a bowl of gold foil chocolate eggs on the coffee table between us. She kicks off a slipper and tucks her bare foot beneath her   body.

The room is filled with pictures, mainly photographs of a man and a boy I take to be her son and his child. There is an easy chair and a television. The TV is recessed in an awkward niche, like a closet without doors. She says she does not like to have the TV as the centerpiece of the room. The room looks like a meditation space with a TV stuck in the corner.

She likes her job very much. She has a curious mind and knows she is good at it. The value of her job is that she can catch a spy. *It is important to be able to spot someone doing something they are not supposed to. Everyone is trying to benefit their own country, but they cannot just do whatever they want in this one.*

The Redacted Manuscript

105

.

It's hard to talk to you. It's a test for me. I am loyal and that makes it hard to talk to you.

If this is the case, I wonder why she is talking to me at all.

She says she feels more Dutch when she is abroad. She , trained classically at the gymnasium, . She wanted to be a doctor but the schooling took too long, the chemistry was too hard. Languages suited her better.

. At the Organization she was the first and only official translator.

.

Her husband moved with her from where she had been studying to the Netherlands and they had a baby. When her son was and two-and-a-half she told him, *Please move on*. They broke up. He stayed on in the country

.

Then she met her second husband.
    . He struggled with the fact that she worked at the Organization. He did not like how she could not discuss her work with him. She had a colleague in the '80s whose wife never knew where he worked. *I don't find it strange that he did not speak about work. It was like he had a cover.*

People stop asking questions once they figure out where she works.

.

She likes to talk. *I am a talkative person.* But she has become a very good listener, she says. *I know how to turn a conversation towards the other person.* She gets pleasure from having company, so she doesn't mind listening rather than talking. *If I talk it's just small talk.*

(Like this.)

.

In the service, *there is a difference between need-to-know and nice-to-know.* Need-to-know is information an agent must have to continue his task; nice-to-know is gossip.

When she took the job she knew it might be dangerous, but it never scared her. She had one colleague who would smoke ten cigarettes before knocking on a door. He did not last long.

She doesn't watch TV. Working at the Organization keeps her fully informed. *What you see on TV is rubbish*. They all say this. *We have to keep the secrets between us. I can't blame the networks; they think they know the truth but they don't.*

The Organization defends democracy.

. *We do the best job we can. We uphold the law.*

.

Her mother was raised *severely Catholic*. Because of that she abandoned religion. Her father was agnostic and her husband was a   orthodox. Her son was baptized in her husband's church. *They did not just sprinkle him with water but completely submerged him.*

She sees a communion between all religions. *Organized religion can force you in a direction you might not want to go*. She has seen religious conservatives and fanatics. The more she sees, the more similar they seem. *It is impossible to have a real conversation with a fanatic.*

She likes to receive compliments but is not interested in fame.

She likes to read Danielle Steele romance novels.

She likes...

She likes...

She proceeds to tell me about her personal tastes and hobbies for the next half hour. When I try to bring the conversation back to the Organization, she says only that she likes her job, *It's nice*. It's as if she has decided that she has said enough for now but still wants to talk—about what I am not sure. I am getting extremely tired, and it's obvious. She asks if I want more coffee. I do. We go into the kitchen for the third time.

Becoming Tarden

. She starts washing out a coffee mug and asks if I need to use the bathroom before I leave. It's clear we are finished. I tell her I am fine. She offers to drive me to the station.

.

I take the train back to Amsterdam. It is past midnight when I unlock the door and crawl over my suitcases into 's bed.

.

He opens his eyes and looks at me, then closes them again.
What was she like?

.

In the dim light I see him grimace.

?

February 25, 2006. Correspondence with   .

. He tells me that he enjoyed our meeting   that I had asked him some very fundamental questions, and that he hoped we could continue our conversation another time. *I've got the feeling we're not finished yet.* He's been trying to locate a copy of *Cockpit*. He'd read another book by Kosinski but could not recall anything about a hummingbird.

He said he is choosing a code name for me.

February 21, 2006. 5:30-8:30pm.   .
Source: Vincent VI

He sticks in my mind as the most threatening of my sources, and leaves a bad aftertaste. All day I've been imagining an exchange between the two of us in his car, like a scene from a movie. He is the first source with whom I would consider going further—to know what it feels like to be a source he handles—for the sake of the experience. I imagine our actions—even in real life—would feel unreal, as if we were actors.

. Murder would be a game for him, somehow sexual; maybe no one need actually die. He is pure appearance. He wears a near-neon turquoise V-neck sweater with a logo of the same color.

. He is not attractive but he is extremely confident. He was ready to toy with me—he was primed and he knew the rules. *I can say anything I want because you will erase my identity anyway.*

. Once inside, he became an agent in the field.

. *That would be confusing*. The Organization has separate ways of dealing with different types of agents.

. The analyst exploits the information. HUMINT is short for human intelligence, and refers to intelligence gathered by means of interpersonal contact.

The Redacted Manuscript

. This is well received by those from the Middle East.

It's a game, yes. It's a game with serious consequences.

I bring up race, he brings up suicide attacks.

I understand, but I disapprove of the method. I respect that suicide bombers fight for their individual freedom.

My job is to be a mirror, to cause a recognition between an agent and myself.

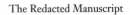

He is cynical about people in general.

He was baptized Roman Catholic and occasionally goes to church.
. After that, he returned to the fundamen-

tals of religion. *I believe in God. I was married in a church.*
He is a liberal; he thinks the government should stay in
the background.

More laissez faire?

Yes, he nods, impressed, as if he did not expect an
American to use a French term.

. *These people will never change.*

.

We are leaning in, towards one another, our elbows
on the table. We both clasp our hands, the fingers of one
dovetailed with the fingers of the other.

I tell him about Tarden, the hummingbird in Kosinski's
book. Tarden goes into a sauna and takes a sword along.
He puts it into a man's anus and forces it all the way up
through his body to his mouth.

. He creates safe situations for himself. He is egotistical. He is at his best when abroad. *Then I have no obligations, no ties. It is the feeling of a life without expectations I am meant to have.*

March 1, 2006.

My list of demands included that I be handled and de-briefed.

Getting handled and debriefed means you're on the other side, no longer the questions but giving over your own personal details and private thoughts. Are you willing to do this? Anyway, I'm interested in getting to know you better.

He promises to look into it and get back to me soon. He bought *Cockpit*, and is still thinking about what my code name should be. He asks that I tell him about myself. *If you tell me something about your own life I'll come up with a name.* It will be a secret name of which I am unaware.

March 7, 2006. Phone call from The Hague to New York.

My contact calls. She and the Committee Head would like to meet with me when I am next in Holland. They are worried about the progress of my assignment. They have been unable to grant me access to some of the people I wish to interview, and want to know how I intend to proceed in light of that. I do not tell her I am sidestepping her, but I am beginning to wonder whether she expects me to do just that, or if someone above her, closer to the center, is hoping that I will.

I tell her I am considering applying to the CIA. She is silent, to which she replies, *If you work for them you can no longer work for us.*

Ten more sources have volunteered. None of them work in

.

We agree that, after my next short visit, I should return to Holland and stay longer.

.

May 20, 2006.   2–5pm. Meeting with contact and
Committee Head.

At first we sit by the front entrance at a large table under the
bar's main chandelier and then relocate to a more private
one in the back corner of the restaurant. The Committee
Head understands that I am frustrated with the limitations
of my position. She poses this as a question.

I tell her that she's correct. I am nowhere, floating
somewhere on the surface of the Organization. They both
shake their heads, visibly frustrated, and tell me that I'm
wrong; I do not realize how deep inside I am, or how vulnerable my position is. I am a liability.

The Committee Head clarifies the structure of the
Organization: *There are seven directions. In those directions
there are teams, and each team has a subject.*

                                        *. There are
only two ministries in the country that take care of vetting—
the Organization and the Ministry of Defense.* Every single
person with whom they work needs to be vetted. They are
constantly adding people to the list; vetting procedures are
always underway. *There is a backlog.*

The Committee that she heads handles the bureaucracy between the Organization and me. It mediates our
relationship, and establishes what is and isn't feasible. She
sees my frustration with the bureaucracy as a direct criti-
cism of her performance.

                    . I feel like I am in a Kafka novel.

                                 .

She explains that she got me inside the Organization on certain conditions. Now I want to change those rules, and that is not possible. She will try to help me by taking me to the Director, but I should expect a negative response.

. I shrug and ask, if that is the case, why let me in at all. They respond that I was hired to reveal the human face of the Organization and the motivations of the people who work there.

.

We are at an impasse, practically arguing but trying to remain controlled. We want the same thing: a successful assignment. I look to my contact to offer me support. I can see that she is trying, but there is only so much she can do.

For a successful assignment, I tell the Committee Head, they will need to trust me.

With all due respect, that is impossible, she responds. *The bottom line is we don't trust anybody. Your position as a personal data consultant was agreed upon as encompassing your collection of personal data and the motivations of your sources. This means you cannot gain further access into our methods or our procedures.*

.

Meeting with the Director.

It is the second time I am truly inside the Building, through
the second façade. My Committee Head leads me through
its maze. It is quiet, muffled. Everything looks the same,
the offices, the cubicles—all dull grey, white, and mint
green except for heavy red curtains at the windows. The
curtains, incongruous with rest of the office décor, surprise
me. We sit for ten minutes in a small waiting room outside the Director's office. A secretary finally calls us, and
my Committee Head and I enter together. We each take
a couch. He addresses me but I hardly speak—it is clear I
am not there to talk but to listen. He speaks to me authori-
tatively, as if I am a child, and yet he is unclear. He speaks
above me, in a condescending tone, in the abstract. I forget
almost all of what he says as soon as he says it.

There is a vitrine in his office filled with gifts from other
countries like ceramic plates, vases, sculptures, trophies,
and knickknacks. I want to put something in it. A glass
paperweight sits on a thin table between the couches, a series
of glass bubbles, each within the one before, three bubbles
in all. *The outer bubble is the Organization, the middle one is our
tools and methods, and at the center is the source,* he tells me.

He denies my request to be trained.

May 23, 2006.   The Hague Station. 2–7:06pm.
Source: Vincent VIII

He is a team leader, and used to be a handler. I try to imagine what he looked like when he was younger—he tells me he was a ladies' man. Sitting across from me here, I think he kind of looks like

. His eyes shift to the door whenever someone enters the bar. When he sees that I notice and follow his gaze, he shrugs. *It's an occupational hazard.*

We both have a cappuccino then move on to white wine. He puts away two glasses and I sip my second slowly. The waitress brings us bowl after bowl of nuts. After we've talked for five hours his speech is more relaxed, he is animated. He leans in and says with a wink, *So you want the informal stuff?*

Yes, that is what I want. Otherwise I know nothing.

His most exciting time at the Organization was when he worked as a handler. *A handler is a lone wolf. It's an addiction, but you get to a point where you tire of it.* Back then he loved recruiting and handling. He also taught how to train as well as an audio and video class.

Many people who enter the Organization have a hard

time accepting the anonymity.

. He likes the thrill of not sleeping, of being in the thick of it, knowing he will change the course of the story.

He considers himself left wing.

. He identifies with the lower middle class and cares most deeply for them.

He likes his job. He enjoys the classified work—*It's like sitting in the first row at the theater.* He's got some French revolution ideas. *Rich and well-organized people have their own politics.* He's playing a game of hide-and-seek with the intelligence world

.

He was part of the BVD, the Binnenlandse Veiligheidsdienst or Domestic Security Service—the name of the Organization before it was rechristened the AIVD.

.

He compares the CIA to the Organization, saying, *The CIA are cowboys.*

If they are cowboys, I ask, then what are you?

We're shepherds.

The Redacted Manuscript

. As for me, my girlfriend makes my clothes so I always look a bit strange.

.

Being a handler can damage your personal life. *I don't like to talk too much, so I'm not a typical handler. We are lone wolves. You have to be OK with being alone nights and weekends, and be fully responsible for your own actions. It's a good feeling but there comes a time when you get fed up with the nomadic life. You are on the road a lot, moving from team to team.*

The agent handler is steered by the Desk Officer, who is the spider in the web. He sends the story to the analyst, who is essentially the storyteller.

Inflated egos are common. If you don't watch yourself, you will start to think you are important. You feel like you have the spotlight, but you are just part of a performance. Agents abroad can feel like they are working autonomously, as they're isolated from the team—this is a dangerous trap for liaison officers.

He once trained

. In one scenario

Everyone thought we were crazy.

When you have a secret, you are the owner of that information. You have to decide what to do with it. You do not necessarily have to share it.

May 24, 2006.   The Hague. 3–6:30pm.
Source: Vincent VII

I am standing at the front entrance of The Hague Central Station, by the taxi rank. He drives up in a   climbs out and leaves the car running, and walks straight over to me. He is tall and thin, with white sideburns and a puff of fine brown hair that rises from the center of his head like a cone. He recognized me—he saw me outside the Building a few days ago. He must have been watching from the window.

We get in his car and drive towards the city center. I study his hands on the steering wheel. His fingers are medium sized, without any rings. They look manicured, but I doubt it.

We leave the car in an underground parking garage beneath the main square. We walk to a bar. Everything he orders I order, one drink after his. I have a cognac at 4 in the afternoon.

His task within the Organization is to visualize all invisible threats. He works with critical infrastructures and key assets.

               —and three causes of disaster: acts of God, technical failures,

              . His job is to identify these threats and inform the public about them.

            . *Onzicht-baar* means 'not visual' in Dutch. He says, *You and I have the same task: to visualize the invisible.*

. He speaks clearly and precisely, gesturing smoothly with his hands. I like him in the same way that I might trust a familiar newscaster on a reputable station—somewhat blindly. He's appropriately animated. When he thinks, he sits back and locks his fingers behind his neck. The hair on the back of his neck is nothing like that on his head—it's curly and coarse, like pubic hair. I watch him toy with it while he speaks.

he wrote a letter to the Organization saying he could be helpful to them. He wrote, *I would like to offer my expertise in the area of national security.* He listed eleven instances of potential terrorist threats and targets in this open letter. They called him soon after. *At thirty-eight years old*, he says proudly, *I transformed my career.*

·

The most extreme change in his personal life since moving   to the Organization is that conversations about work now take two minutes instead of two hours. His old job required that he tell the whole story. Now, he cannot even tell a fraction of it.

I ask him where I am in this story.

Even if I gave you one small detail, you wouldn't know where to place it. It would be one piece in a puzzle of a thousand.

How many puzzle pieces do I currently have?

I'd estimate that you have several little islands of the whole puzzle assembled, each made up of ten to twenty pieces. That's pretty good. You know a lot.

What do I know?

What do you think you don't know?

I am looking for the center, the face of the Organization.

There is no face. We simply have bigger ears, and larger eyes to look through, we have lenses, we have antennae, we have a special computers in our heads that and can look exactly where you am looking but see so much more.

. He smiles at this. I smile too. *Its selection and extraction raises it to this level.*

Labeling information as secret material makes it valuable. Categorizing information as secret is the best was to make it consumable. *Information only becomes information when it is consumed.*

The biggest secret of the secret service is that you don't know if there is a secret.

The Organization, he says, is always subject to speculation. *You must prove that the white raven does not exist. The human brain is good at nourishing the conspiracy theory. What the Organization wants the most is that it remains speculation.* The secret itself is much more beautiful that its revelation.

In this world we have a need for fantasy and speculation. Information is the central backbone of society. In the old world, we relied on the existence of God and the mystery of his infrequent appearances. And when God no longer appeared, other media did. Perhaps conspiracy theories are the visualization of God through other media. We used to see only signs, such as miracles or the Virgin Mary, suggesting the presence of God. Information replaces God as the mechanism, but part of the system remains secret. We see only fragments. It's about perspective: You can see there is a secret from the outside but, when you are inside of it, you cannot see it because you are in it.

He explains that you need special resources to visualize threats that the public cannot see, otherwise they remain invisible. *There is a tension. You need special tools, human sources like* HUMINT—a syllabic abbreviation of the words human intelligence referring to intelligence gathered by means of interpersonal contact, *or technological sources like* SIGNINT—*taps and mics etcetera. But you can only use them once you can prove there is a threat—or a potential threat.* This developmental stage is the grey area—you need information to prove that you need to get more information.

The ideal source is an open person who will share all their thoughts on their personal data with those around them, and at the same time know when to be discreet. A lot of friends is a good indicator but, once they're in, as an agent in the field, those friends become a problem, especially for their handlers.

At the Organization, they look out for telltale signs.

you have to put your mind inside that of a terrorist. *You have to force yourself to feel able—and willing—to do violent things. You must suppose that your only mission is to harm people.* You must focus on the negative and dangerous people who are not open to debate or discussion. Ninety-nine percent of the human population does not want to overthrow public freedom.

. There are no James Bonds—not a lot of cash and no fancy cars.

. *Informers are not one hundred percent convinced they are running with the right crowd from the start. They are ninety percent convinced—we get them there, and pull them back to our side—the side of democracy. They are smart enough to recognize that another Hitler or Osama Bin Laden is not the answer.*

I tell him being a handler sounds interesting to me, and ask if it does to him.

He sits back with his hands behind his neck and his eyebrows arched high. He says he knows he is good at getting information. He knows how to talk to people. He has the ability to pull information out of people, to make connections, to see the bigger picture. But it's a choice to put oneself in that position, to collect information from an agent in the field. It's a choice that he, personally, has decided not make.

May 25, 2006.   The Hague. 4–8pm.
Source: Miranda IV

The café is extremely crowded. I'm early. I lean up against the large glass cake display case by the register and doodle on café postcards. I didn't want to come this time. They are starting to repeat one another.

.

Personal information is only interesting if it becomes a threat.

.

I ask her what constitutes a blackmail-worthy secret.

The meeting takes four long hours, each one heavy and full of bitterness. When I leave, I feel as trapped as she does. I no longer want to be an agent handler. It is tiring to talk for so long with someone in whom, in any other circumstance, I would take no interest. I have to listen and pretend to care. Maybe I am hungry, or maybe my sources are boring and have little to offer. Afterwards I feel empty, as if I need to cry.

May 25, 2006.
Source: Vincent IX

I am   café, waiting for my source. I know he is very tall and older than most of them I've met. I look around the room and make eye contact with various men. Ten minutes go by. One man is sitting at the large communal table, reading the newspaper. He looks tall even sitting. He looks up at me over the edge of the paper numerous times. I stare back. I wonder if he is the one, and if he is, why he doesn't acknowledge me.

. I am clearly
distracted as we greet each other, but he is caught up in his
own world and does not notice. I let him speak and nod
my head as I look around cautiously.

.

The source walks in hurriedly, passes by me, and abruptly realizes his mistake. *Are you Jill?* he asks.

.

We go up to the second floor balcony where it's quieter.
He begins with orange juice, switches to Coca-Cola, and
finishes with coffee. He orders two of each, as if a ghost is
sitting with us at the table.

He keeps taking my pen from me and adding notes to
my book. He says he does not want to give me a lecture
about the history of Islam but repeatedly gives me a lecture
about the history of Islam. Each time he begins this speech,
he confiscates the pen.

. He calls himself an elder. He thinks he is older
than he is.

His clothes are put together funnily, like a secondhand suit in a thrift shop. All his garments are part of the
same color family—a pale green misty grey—but they
don't belong in the same outfit. The suit jacket is some
kind of fake tweed.

. He speaks with un-
bending authority and assurance. He looks the part of the
behind-the-scenes authority figure, the iconic criminal
administrator. It's the kind of man you can only imagine
being this age and in this position, as if he was were born
for this role. He truly believes in what he does. And he
tells me that what he does: is *to produce freedom. Protecting
freedom is to produce it.*

The most important thing is to look through the eyes
of the target—to see his story, his history, and the reasons
for his behavior.

? *Now I am looking at you, and wondering how
to see through the eyes of a young artist.*

He brought me a book. It's in Dutch and filled with
images of ancient Greek and Egyptian artwork.

His job is to understand other people's perceptions,
their sensitivities. He is starting to remind me of my old
boyfriend—he has his pretension but also the wherewithal
to back it up. I have to give it to him. He earned it, even if
it pisses me off.

.

His parents were Catholic, and he still retains traces
of this history even though he moved beyond it long ago.
His work is to protect democracy so that those weaker than
himself can be free.

This guy should be cast in bronze.

He likes to tell me about his *marginal friends*:

! It's like a politically correct sitcom with all the 'others' represented.

At this point he takes my pen again and moves my book in front of him. I try to stay calm through my anger. Give me back my book.

He has since learned to be invisible, to be unknown

. These days he speaks only through the mouth of Seibren, the director of the Organization. Only two of his friends know where he works.

.

He always questions whether he can trust people. He knows that, as an individual, you can only contribute a little. Famous people can influence others, but a novel can change the world.

It takes six or seven months to get to know a person, and even longer to really know them. To truly know a person you have to see them under stress. He looks at the individual, not the institution of which they are a part. To understand a person, he goes to those who are close to him. If he wanted to know about me he would start with my mother. He would approach her and say he was a friend of mine. *All mothers*

Becoming Tarden

love to talk about their children.

One can always know too much information. *You cannot be candid at the Organization, even with your partner. You have to keep it all inside.* For security reasons, you need to stay silent. Releasing sensitive information can have disastrous consequences.

and, by doing so, his service produces freedom for an open society. *It's not just security and it's not just preventing terrorism.* The more forthcoming you are, the more questions you are asked. *"Better not to know," as the elders say.* If you know something you are responsible for it. Know what you need to know, and not more, so you can sleep better.

May 27, 2010.   Leiden.
Source: Vincent X

He is already there when I arrive and recognizes me immediately. He gets up from the bar, holding his drink, and walks me to a table.

I am surprised—he looks and sounds American, as if

144

he just stepped out of an LL Bean catalogue.

. He says he is not neat and organized and that I would discern that immediately upon visiting his house. I wouldn't guess that from what he is wearing.

He is responsible for the practice of clustering knowledge of people together, so that his department can get through the backlog of pending cases faster and more easily. He will not explain exactly what clustering means, but he will tell me how it is he vets people.

"Your face is burned." That means your face is known, and so is your identity. When your face is burned, you can no longer be operational. As an agent, you are diffused.

He wishes he had known about me sooner as he would

have arranged for me to be interviewed. He even knows who should do it. I want them to come to my house and try to disturb my life. I say he can do it this week and tell him my free days.

No, he says, *it doesn't work like that. We are booked up for weeks. You have to plan ahead.*

I tell him I will, and resolve to arrange this with my contact.

.

He thinks of the Organization as male.

To do interviews you must be a mirror, objective. It's a matter of role-playing. *You have to posit an opinion without really feeling it, without getting personally involved.*

.

Interlude

I return to New York once again.

.

147

December 16, 2006.

June 10, 2006.
Source: Vincent XI

The airport is packed with moving people. I head to the meeting point as planned and stand there, waiting to be recognized. I still find it a funny feeling to stand still waiting for a stranger, knowing that somebody in this pedestrian mass will seek me out, come to me, and tell me it is he, the person for whom I am waiting.

He suggests we go upstairs to the café on the viewing deck. We pick a small, secluded table by the window, past the giant buffet island. We keep the red plastic tray on which we carried our coffee to the table. He seems innocuous. He wears a long-sleeved black button-down shirt over a grey T-shirt, black jeans, and black shoes.

. If people want more, they have to give more. And you need to be very specific with what you ask for; no one voluntarily shares information.

It is not his job to ask questions—it's to file and send.

.

He protects his face from getting burned in case he

decides to go operational. This means he never allows people to photograph his face.

Politically, he is right of the center.

He likes to watch people   .

Getting security clearance was exciting for him. Since then he's felt validated, like his life so far has been OK.

I am weary and have finished my second cup of coffee. It's like I am listening to elevator music, a loop of the same endless song, and I can't turn it off. Each time I dig for something unusual about his role or new informative about the Organization,

                    . It is silly to press him for answers that I know he can't provide.

I thank him for his time. He looks at me expectantly.

But wait, you did not ask me personal questions.

I tell him that's OK, I have what I need.

He insists. *But I thought you were going to inquire about my personal life. I will answer anything you ask! Don't you want to know?*

I tell him I am no longer asking those questions, and repeat that I already have what I need.

He refuses to let it go, or to let me go. I realize he has turned the tables on me. I am even a bit rude. I know most people would just leave, but I feel responsible.

Fine, I say, tell me your personal data. I sit back down and make a list of the five categories in Article 12: religion, convictions on life, race, health and sexual life. I begin with the second.

Convictions on life:
To celebrate life, sense of humor…

He lists off generic responses, not worth repeating here. There is nothing further to pursue. Annoyed and feeling through with this, I thank him for the third time and close my book. He persists. *Don't you want to know more personal things?*

It would seem you have something you want to tell me, so why don't you just tell me?

He looks nervous.

I ask if he needs to confess.

No, he says, but then thinks for a moment and says, *Well, maybe. Yes.* Taking this as license, he proceeds.

He continues, filling the space between us with words.

I am becoming claustrophobic, almost crazy, and it empowers me to ask him anything, as if there are no boundar-

ies, a wild and violent free-for-all. I am not nervous, as I
have been with some of my other sources.

. I am his platform, and it is
my fault. I set myself up for this.

Please keep going.

What do you want me to find? Tell me what to dig up.
Do you still need to confess?

No.

Are you sure?

.

I stand up.

.

I pack my bag.

. My reaction is bigger than
Vincent XI, or any one source, but rather all of them com-
bined and my relation to them. It's as if, by taking on the
position of a handler, I have disparaged myself.

July 4, 2006.   .

2007. The Hague.

My visits to Holland in March and July are for mainte-
nance and clarification. Meetings are isolated to within the
Building. I oscillate between

for twenty minute interviews, with fifteen-minute breaks in between. The sessions generally run over, giving me no rest at all. To maintain their anonymity, my sources wait to exit their respective rooms until they hear the door of the other meeting room close. To be sure, they can peek out and check the red light above the other meeting room is on. . All my meetings are now scheduled through the Committee Head. I have requested to see only those sources left on my waiting list, and those with whom I have outstanding business. I no longer feel emotionally involved but simply need them to fill in the gaps. I make a point to schedule an appointment with any of my sources whose face is unclear in my memory or my notes and observe them well.

March 20, 2007.   . 20 minutes.
Source: Vincent V

.

'Personal' is my job, I say. I suggest that he photocopies the relevant pages and gives them to me with whatever he doesn't want me to read whited-out, just as the Organization does.

.

That you do not drink alcohol.
That's a big assumption to make from one cup of tea.
Yes, it would be.

.

Same day, 20 minutes later.   .
Source: Vincent IX

.

She keeps my schedule in her notebook and lays it open on
the table so I can see it

and he says, *No. Officially, you
don't exist here.*

The Redacted Manuscript

March 24, 2006.

but then goes silent on me. When I call to get the meeting point, there is no answer. I never hear from him again.

July 10, 2006.   .
Source: Vincent X

I meet with Vincent X again

. He informs me that permission has been denied.

. Usually he knows how to talk to people on the outside to whom he would tell nothing, like his neighbor, but it is more complicated with me. He also notes that all of the information he has given me is publicly available. Frustrated, I ask how my position is at all different from anyone else's. He says that it is very different: I have spent time inside the Organization, talked to sources on numerous occasions, in depth and for hours at a time. He reiterates: *You have our faces—not only what we look like but our motivations, our feelings, our pasts.*

Yes, I say, I can burn you.

He smiles, knowing that he taught me this term.

Yes, I can burn them, and to burn them is to destroy them, to diffuse them and let them go. Looking at his smug expression,

. I can only respond to the Organization using the one freedom it has allotted me—observing the faces I found in it.

November 7, 2007. New York.

It has been almost two years since I began my assignment with the Organization and five months since my last meeting with a source. My report is nearing completion, and yet it feels unfinished. I feel unfinished. I do not know what I am missing—only that it is the very thing I have been looking for. I call my Committee Head, make the necessary arrangements, and plan my return to Holland two weeks from today.

November 27, 2007. The Hague. 5:30pm. Committee Head.

I meet my Committee Head in an espresso bar a few blocks from The Hague Central Station for a short meeting about pragmatics. Business is done quickly and we have some time

to chat. I ask her the whereabouts of a few of my sources. She has to think about it carefully. Some of the names I'd been given, she tells me, were not their real names (I only knew them by their first names). I ask about Vincent IV,
. She squints her eyes, confused. *Which one is he?*

Later.   , The Hague. 6:45pm.
Source:

He is my beginning and my end, and everything in between was a way to connect the two.

He arrives after me and asks if I've been waiting long. I haven't. He's wearing a similar suit the one he always wears. This one is dark blue with white pinstripes.

. He thinks the café's too crowded, so we leave.

. It's designed like an old-style brown bar. We move to the back to a small narrow room of candlelit tables, as far from the bar as possible. He removes his tie while standing. As he sits down, he neatly folds it in three and places it in the left breast pocket of his suit jacket. I want to ask if I can have it. It is the silkiest thing that I have seen him wear,   . I hold back, but my desire persists throughout dinner.

          . He says the food is not so good here but that dinner is on him, and touches his hand to his chest.

He asks how I have been and how the assignment is progressing. I inform him that, finally, it is almost over; he is my last appointment.

Do I take it, he asks as he leans in to pick up his wine glass, *that it was not a good experience?*

No, that is not what I meant. It was a difficult experience, but it was what it was.

He is talking about the bourgeoisie when he interrupts himself to comment on my ring. It's a cameo. I cannot recall if he went to touch it, but he did lean forward to have a closer look. I give him the ring to inspect, and he studies the lady in profile. He thinks she is clumsily carved, her chin pointy and her eyes deeply recessed, but that her hair is romantic. He motions to his own face while describing hers, and then looks up at me. He uses her romanticism as a metaphor for mine.

He asks me why I choose to make the work I do.

To reveal something. To find clarity, truth, or love.

What about fear?

I tell him that fear is a part of love, as well as the capacity to sense fear and to choose to move towards it. It is the ability to be vulnerable, to love in light of the risk of pain. He says he finds it difficult working so closely to terrorist sects. There is a lot of fear and vulnerability within them. *It is difficult for those inside to trust one another.* And it is scary for him because the more time he spends watching them the more he begins to understand them. He asks me if I know what agent loving is.

I do.

I bring up Israel and Palestine, and how I find it hard to believe that one side is good and one is bad. I am more interested in the emotions and living conditions that drive people to strap bombs to their bodies.

I ask him what he means. He says the higher the stakes, the more the secret needs to be protected. And the bigger the secret the harder it is to contain. *It isn't human nature to keep secrets. Someone will always let it slip.* Someone gets lazy, words always leak.

. He never used to feel secure in hotel rooms when he was traveling, but he feels safer now that he rationalizes it this way.

We finish our meal and move to the smoking section near the bar. He orders us cognac and espressos, and pulls an open pack of cigarettes from his pocket.

He morphs in front of me by the minute. My perception of him changes so much that I keep losing him and re-recognizing him. Although he's only four years older than me, I feel like a child in comparison. He is big, heroic, iconic, like a superhero action figure. I tell him this and he blushes.

You didn't get what you wanted?

I am not sure I got deep enough. I had wanted to go deeper.

Do you think you've failed?

No. I found what you let me find, perhaps more, and I took it as far as I could.

I relay my experiences since I saw him last: Initially, I was frustrated. The Organization felt like a white, engulfing fog. The Organization had put me in a box but I couldn't see it. I thought to describe the fog—

Too easy.

I know. I wanted to move inside, past the fog, as far as I could go. I used Article 12 as my way in. I thought that by knowing a number of individuals within the Organization personally I would come to understand the Organization as a whole, and find the face at its center. You hired me to make something for you and the Organization, to represent you in a positive light,

. He complains that those in liberal positions often think they are on the left but, in reality, they are conservatively liberal.

I sketch the path of my trajectory into the Organization with my fingers on the table. He listens, but interrupts so many times that the line I attempt to draw is broken into pieces. We work through each person I met.

Any women?

Yes,

—

How many people?

.

And you got all that?

You're good.

. I describe my search for the center, how my sources seemed like decoys. I admit that, at the start, I thought perhaps there was no center, and that if I got to know my sources I would come to know the system—

.

His words fall like weights upon the table. They echo, dark and hollow. I pause and hold his gaze before continuing. But since the sources guarded this center so determinedly, I began to think that perhaps it did exist after all. He frowns.

. *They give the system a center because that is how they function within it, as its servers.*

He is different. He embodies the system. He understands what he is. He says this and I believe him. He is the center simply because he can see it. My center, the one I sought but could not see, flickered before me like a dying star. I fluctuated between believing in it and doubting its existence, at one moment seeing it as an illusion my sources were perpetuating, and at another as something tangible and real.

: Even an illusion becomes reality when enough people call it truth. They make it real.

I spoke with the minor people. You are the highest-ranking person I have met.

Yes.

And then you fell away and the rest of my assignment

was a journey back to you. That is why we are here now. I needed to see you again, last. It was intuition. You debrief me, and I'll debrief you.

Yes.

He asks me if I even know what he does at the Organization. I do.

. He is also my favorite spy.

I am not a spy, he says.

I tell him, I call all of you my spies.

He laughs and takes a drag of his cigarette.

. He has to train those below him, and give them room to make mistakes so they can learn. Only when they are in a position where they cannot afford to screw up does he say, *OK, now we have to do this.* Otherwise he tries to let people find their own way. He wants them to be free-thinking and creative so they will improve.

I ask if he is doing this with me.

No. He says it immediately. *I am giving you something so that I can get something back.* He wants to fill in my gaps. He wants me to be a mirror—of both himself and the Organization. He wants to see through me into where he is.

Do you have any questions?

Yes. What do you want from me?

He wonders what I would be if I was not an artist. He thinks a fundamental scientist.

He goes to the bar and brings back two liqueurs, of

slightly different colors, and asks me to choose one. I take
the light-colored one in the girly glass. We are sitting at
a table in the smoking section, cut off from the bar by a
heavy curtain. The mood is so intense that I see nothing
behind him, feel nothing beyond us. It is only later, when
we notice the waiter stacking chairs on empty tables that
we realize everyone has left except a few drunken regulars
at the bar.

        . Cigarette butts spill from the ashtray. We buy
another pack.

I tell him about Vincent XI and my experience with
him at   .

Agents, he says, *take longer to cultivate than you had. Do
you think all vetting procedures are done like that?* He asks me
again with the stern force of a teacher, giving away more
than he thinks I already know.

But, I say, I was not vetting him. Vetting is an internal
process. You are vetted to get inside the system, and he
already was. By then I was acting as an agent handler
rather than a data collector, seeking information about the
Organization's methods and the power at its center. I soon
realized that he was not going to be able to provide me
with this information. He was a potential source who had
no useful information to offer. I tried to excuse myself but
he turned the tables on me.

And what did you learn from that about our organization?

168

Nothing. I learned about my methodology. He confronted me there and then. He did to me what I have been doing. He was promised a structure, a system—to have his personal data collected—and I did not do what he expected. I did not give him what he had volunteered for, so he demanded it of me. I was confronted with the position I had put others in. And I had put myself there. It was a terrible experience, but an important one.

He leans towards me, raising a finger in front of his face. *If you meet with ten sources you are lucky to find even one with the information you need.*

There isn't a word for what I feel sitting there with him. Love comes closest, but it is not love laced with sex—though our sexual desire peeks through at times. I do not feel it as much as think it. The desire to be inside him and have him inside of me is not physical but metaphysical. I feel love in all its various definitions—as recognition, as a catalyst for becoming, as a revelation, but not as a resolution. It's like a pair of facing mirrors that open up one another, extending space endlessly—not an illusion but a visceral experience. I did find the center, a center reflected in one of its parts.

How could you still believe there was a center after meeting all these people?

I move on to Vincent X   —

He has not been part of the Organization long.

I know.

. That was when I most clearly sensed you'd drawn the line.

He furrows his brow,

.

I know.

. I was frustrated
with all the boundaries.
We feared that might happen.

.

He says it is hard for him to hear my opinions about
the Organization because he wants to believe he works
for a good, smart system. I tell him my understanding of the system is dependent upon whom and what I
was given.

He interjects in his coaching voice: *Let's say you work
for us at a university campus* (he mumbles something about
tracing the 9/11 hijackers to the University of Hamburg)
*and you get a call that two students might be planning some-
thing—an attack, perhaps. You are given their names and phone
numbers. What do you do first?* I am excited he is training
me. At that moment he receives a phone call he says he
needs to take. I use the time to think. When he is off the
phone, I tell him I would google them. He rolls his eyes. I
backtrack. I mean, I would begin that way—

No. He traces the movements I should make. The first
thing I should do is check the Organization's archives to
see if their names are already in the system. *We have a lot
of archives.*

When they are ready to move in on someone, the
Organization's first priority is to get the source out safely.

. They are inevitably betraying someone, and they nearly always have a reason to do so.

.

The danger of the system, even in a democracy, he says, *is that people become too comfortable within its structure and get lazy. There is a lack of personal responsibility.* He is referring to my sources,   .
They feign an open, liberal point of view but are not really aware and question nothing. They pretend to be liberal but are in fact full of prejudice. *An open society demands an active consciousness, constant debate.*

The danger for an empire or a communist state—or even a democracy gone awry—is that the people with power and those without are pushed farther apart. And the people on the inside become more cruel to those on the outside for fear of becoming one of them.

. If the Organization were so removed from society he would not choose to be a part of it. He wants to be invested in society.

I believe him. I am sitting across from him trying to fight it, struggling against my trust in him, holding on to

171

the fictions I have read and the idea of 'the other.' Believing him threatens my position as a critical listener—and my desire for a secret to actually exist. It threatens the safety of knowing that I am on one side of the line and he is on the other. Without that line, it is hard to define where we both stand. But the world from which Kosinski came, fearful of communism and fascism, is not the one in which we live now. *Holland*, he reiterates, *is small*. Its secrets are relatively minor, even though the Organization wields a greater international influence by means of its methods (with which he is involved). I wish they were bigger. But I also want to hear him without judgment, to let my fears go, to not worry that everything that has come before this was part fantasy, and that my desire to believe in that fantasy is perhaps even more complicated than the truth I seek itself.

He breaks into my thoughts like a drill sergeant. He does not let my mind wander or get carried away. He asks me a simple, cutting question: *Why do you think we keep secrets?*

Because this is a game in which people barter with secrets, so you have to have them too.

He nods.

I preface that what I am about to ask him may sound naïve, but… Might there be a way to neutralize the game? What would happen if one team refused to play? Or better yet, kept playing but changed the rules? If the Organization—just for instance—continued its work but did so transparently, keeping secrets would have no value. The constant exchange between nations—a tit for tat—could no longer be engaged.

He lets me finish, and then continues without comment.

We are not the heroes, he says. *Our sources are. They are the ones who have to betray. It is rarely one of us playing that role.* He has never had a real conversation with a terrorist.

Never?

No, never.

Again, I want to believe he is wrong, that they are driven by passion or the belief that they can start a revolution. He says no, they are just compensating for something.

He worries that I am disappointed, that I am bored with the Organization and him for not giving me what I want. But I am just as interested in the boringness of it. He smiles and says he likes that—and for a moment he seems smaller. A bunch of ordinary people meeting me at Burger King, mall cafeterias, airport meeting points. Some of us sharing the desire for it to be more important, more dangerous, more suspiscious than it is: to be inside the action, closer to the center. But our insignificance stays the same. Yes. The game is played by all of us. The drama depends upon the illusion that there is something greater than we are at play—strange, powerful, even threatening—with the answers hidden safely at its center while we, alone, stand outside of it.

Secrets are dangerous. If you wear a mask there must be a moment of unmasking.

He does not want to come off as arrogant, but he is one of the conscious ones. He is well informed and bears responsibility for his position.

Where he comes from he is the black sheep for joining the Organization. Now he wears the black sheep's clothing.

I ask him about   . He cannot place him in his mind's eye. I describe him and he remembers. I need him. He has my codename.

But you would never know your codename.

Yes, but I would when I was done and had handed everything over to the Organization, including my original files.

No. You would still never know it.

The ancient Chinese believed that when people are startled awake from a deep sleep their souls could get caught in the dream world, lost from their body. To get your soul back someone has to whisper your name into your ear, calling it home, out from the dream world and into your body.

You would never hear it. Use that. If your soul is not called back, you are lost.

I *am* lost.

That is also interesting.

I am his sincere experiment. I chose him and he chose me.

We were worried that you would not be able to get what you needed. We could foresee that you would want more than you could have, and that we would have to limit you. We gave you a difficult task—perhaps an impossible one. I want to give you now as much as I can. This is all between us, of course.

This is the moment I give in. I have no choice but to

trust him, to tell the truth completely, to lay down all my cards. He is the one with whom I stop playing the game. For Kosinksi's protagonist, there was no way to step outside the system. I maintain the illusion that I can.

I explain my perception of the Director of the Organization as hovering above the center. When I met with him in his office I could not understand him.

. He spoke to me as if I were a child, and even then it was incomprehensible. My eyes wandered around his office to the thick red curtains and the sculpture on his desk, the bubbles within bubbles. He explained its symbolism to me, the layers of the Organization with the fragile, crystal-clear source as the nucleus in the center.

Some of the questions I had for him no longer seem important. I forget to ask him about the charts.

. I fear I've been betrayed. Is he just another source who has changed his name?

.

The bar is closing. We put out our cigarettes, he pays the check, and we leave the restaurant. His bicycle is outside, parked in the square.

. I have always wanted one. He unchains it from the metal post and says,   . I jump on the back and wrap my arms around his waist. I press myself against his body as he bikes us to the station. Holding him like this—my face resting on his shoulder, my fingers spread between the thick folds of his woolen coat— is intimate. Yet I feel something else. The tension between us is undeniable—we bike in relative silence—but it is not sexual. When he asks if I am comfortable, I feel his voice in his back as it vibrates through his chest.

We arrive. He locks his bike to a rack and escorts me into the station. It is almost empty. *Oh no*, he says, as we approach the departure board. The next train to Amsterdam Central Station is at 1:27am, half an hour from now. It's OK, I tell him. I feel wide-awake and high, and I don't need him to stay. It is the first time I have felt alive and free from the Organization since I began this. It's as if I am living an ending here in this freezing cold station, standing before the departure board that lists where I have lived and from where I will leave early tomorrow morning. For the moment I feel satisfied. Fragments of our dinner conversation flash back. I talked of love and he spoke of fear and asked why I make the work I do. *What is the point?* I have no point, no moral to share. I am not offering him an answer, nor do I expect one from myself. I do not know what I am looking for, but I know when I have found it. I can sense the truth beyond the fog. I feel my blood circulating through my body,   , black as his pupils engulfing his irises—first the blue, then the grey, that delicate boundary between black and white disappeared, and I am there inside it.

He is standing to the side of me. He says he looks forward to reading my report. *You should be critical.*

I thank him for being my favorite spy. He blushes, and turns to face me. We embrace quickly, full of hope and warmth.

Thank you,   for giving me permission.

He nods, then turns away and leaves.

I make my way to the station's Burger King with its spattering of teenagers and drunks. I order a soggy chocolate muffin that I do not eat and a bottle of water, and sit down in one of the restaurant's red plastic booths. I take out my notebook and write down everything I can remember of the evening. I am overwhelmed in this fast-food restaurant, amongst the stale burgers and flat sodas. Through the restaurant's Plexiglas window I watch the trains pull in and out of the station—the same trains that, time and again, have drawn me through the fields and villages of this country. They are as familiar as they are unfamiliar, like walking through New York after finishing a book by Gabriel Garcia Marquez, when the streets I know transform into something else I don't.

I leave the restaurant and walk to track number seven. A faceless yellow train backs down the platform at 1:25am. It sobers me. Shivering, drunk teenagers wait in groups to board. I step up into a beer-filled car. The air is stained with alcohol and sour breath. I feel like the ending of a fiction novel is enclosing me while I am in the real. I think of   , and how my journey has led me back to him. I am in a love story, or a story of love and fear and mirrors, all facing my favorite spy yet reflecting nothing.

Almost an hour passes. Last stop, Amsterdam Central Station. The journey ends as quickly as it began. I am so awake and yet so tired. I get off the train close to 2:30am and use the station bathroom as a dark-skinned man mops the floor outside my stall—he is one of the people who maintain the façade of the busy station, invisible, working at night. Efficient as Holland is, the escalator is operated by sensors. It sits quiet and dead until my foot rises over it, ready to walk down its too-tall metal steps, when it suddenly jerks awake. The steps glide downwards in even succession, carrying me to street level and spitting me out into the damp, black night of the city. My boots resound on the wet, inky pavement, and I hear him speaking to me, like a ghost in my mind. *Will you ever come back here now that you're done with your assignment?* Yes, I tell him. I have to return. But I know I will not come back, not to this same place. Tonight is my finish line, and everything that follows is an epilogue.

If the center were so very different from the periphery, I would not want to be inside of it.

The station is behind me, fading into the fog. I walk towards   's house and watch my reflection in the puddles as I pass beneath the streetlights. I picture   's face. It was more beautiful and awkward than I had recalled. There was a strength to his voice and gestures I had not witnessed before—or he had never shown me. Perhaps it was because it was late and we'd closed down the bar or because we had shared a bottle of red wine and a few cognacs. But I don't think so. I did not feel drunk and he did not appear to be, either. Our eyes were locked, the expectation and desire between us our radar—but not a desire within my lap or my chest, although I was aware of a dull sexual throb. Our sexual attraction was a given, almost a common point of connection that was left unaddressed in place of another, more pressing need to make oneself understood, to be clear, in the knowledge there was no time left. The more we gave to one another within the bounds of our dual identities the riper the fruit, the more intense its texture, the sweeter its taste. He gave me permission and acknowledged that what I write might be harsh, might be angry, but it could never be ugly if it is genuine and authentic and true.

Tell me what you need to know. Tell me what I can tell you.

The city opens up to me. It feels hollow. I was right about his hair. It is a bit longer now, and thinned out like the fine gauze of cotton candy,

. Soft eyebrows, pink rims around his blue eyes that, in the dark bar, looking at me across the table, were totally black—the blue halos completely eclipsed by the open, staring pupils that swallowed me whole. He said he exercises what I called his uptight and conservative stance to offset his liberal past,   and played   ,
unexpected activities he uses to prove to me the vastness of his complexities.

Postscript

On January 4, 2010, two representatives from the AIVD took permanent custody of the unredacted body of the book, *Becoming Tarden*, from my exhibition "Authority to Remove" at the Tate Modern in London. I had exhibited the book according to the suggestions of the Director of the AIVD, as "a visual work of art in a one-time-only exhibition, after which it would become the property of the Dutch government and would be stripped of all sensitive information and not be published." The museum was our dead letter box.

All that time and trouble, and still the record
is a superficial one: I see only how I looked in the
fraction of a second when the shutter was open.
But there's no trace of the thoughts and emotions
that surrounded that moment. When I die and
my memories die with me, all that will remain
will be thousands of yellowing photographs
and 35mm negatives locked in my filing cabinets.

—Jerzy Kosinski, *Cockpit*